Anonymus

Return of judicial Statistics of Ireland, 1894

Anonymus

Return of judicial Statistics of Ireland, 1894

ISBN/EAN: 9783741199820

Manufactured in Europe, USA, Canada, Australia, Japa

Cover: Foto ©Lupo / pixelio.de

Manufactured and distributed by brebook publishing software
(www.brebook.com)

Anonymus

Return of judicial Statistics of Ireland, 1894

CRIMINAL AND JUDICIAL STATISTICS, IRELAND, 1894.

REPORT

ON THE

CRIMINAL AND JUDICIAL STATISTICS OF IRELAND

FOR THE YEAR 1894,

WITH TABLES RELATING TO—

(I.) Police—Crime and its Distribution—Modes of Procedure for Punishment of Crime—Proceedings in Criminal Courts—Persons under Detention in Prisons and other places of Confinement—Cost of the Repression of Crime.

(II.) Civil Proceedings in Supreme Courts of Appeal; the Divisions of the High Court of Justice; the Court of the Irish Land Commission; the High Court of Admiralty; the Court of Bankruptcy; and in Larger and Smaller District Courts—Law Stamps and Taxes—Consolidated Taxing Offices—Registration of Judgments, Titles, Deeds, &c.

Presented to both Houses of Parliament by Command of Her Majesty.

DUBLIN:
PRINTED FOR HER MAJESTY'S STATIONERY OFFICE,
BY ALEXANDER THOM & CO. (LIMITED).

And to be purchased, either directly or through any Bookseller, from
Hodges, Figgis, and Co. (Limited), 104, Grafton-street, Dublin; or
Eyre and Spottiswoode, East Harding-street, Fleet-street, E.C.; or
John Menzies and Co., 12, Hanover-street, Edinburgh, and 90, West Nile-street, Glasgow.

1895.

CHARLEMONT HOUSE, DUBLIN,

2nd September, 1895.

SIR,

I have the honour to submit herewith, for the consideration of His Excellency the Lord Lieutenant, my Report on the Criminal and Judicial Statistics of Ireland for the year 1894, together with the Tables appended thereto.

I remain, Sir,

Your obedient servant,

THOS. W. GRIMSHAW,

Registrar-General.

CONTENTS OF REPORT.

PART I.—CRIMINAL STATISTICS.

CHAPTER III.—CRIMINALS AND OTHERS IN CONFINEMENT, AND KNOWN CRIMINALS AT LARGE.

CHAPTER IV.—COST OF THE REPRESSION OF CRIME.

PART II.—JUDICIAL STATISTICS.

Page

CONTENTS OF APPENDIX OF TABLES.

PART I.—CRIMINAL STATISTICS.

I. POLICE TABLES.

II. STATE PRISONS.

IV. REFORMATORY SCHOOLS.

V. INDUSTRIAL SCHOOLS.

VI. LUNATIC ASYLUMS, AS TO CRIMINAL LUNATICS AND DANGEROUS LUNATICS CHARGED WITH INTENT TO COMMIT A CRIME.

PART II.—JUDICIAL STATISTICS.—CIVIL PROCEEDINGS.

I. CENTRAL ADMINISTRATION OF JUSTICE.

High Court of Justice.

INDEX TO SUBJECTS

IN

REPORT AND TABLES.

CRIMINAL AND JUDICIAL STATISTICS (IRELAND), 1894.

REPORT.

GENERAL REMARKS.

The information dealt with in the following Report was collected in the usual manner, and, as far as possible, has been classified so that it may be in accord with that contained in previous reports upon the same subject. General Remarks.

The Report is, as on former occasions, divided into two principal sections—that relating to the Criminal, and that dealing with the Judicial, Statistics. Each of these portions has been again subdivided so as to allow of the more important items being referred to in detail.

A general review of the tables contained in the Appendix points to the following conclusions:—

1. That there has been a very slight increase (not amounting to 0·5 per cent.) in the total number of Criminal offences and charges in Ireland in 1894, as compared with 1893, the number for which year was 4 per cent. under that for 1892.
2. That both absolutely and in proportion to the estimated population the more serious offences (those not determined summarily) are considerably below the average for the ten years 1884–93, the absolute number being less than the number for any of those years, and the rate based on the estimated population being under that for any of the ten years, except 1892, the rate for which it slightly exceeds.
3. That the less serious offences (those determined summarily) exceed by a small amount the number for the preceding year, and, although in actual number there has been a decrease as compared with the average number for the ten years 1884–93, yet, allowing for the decrease in the population, cases of this nature are relatively somewhat above the average for that period.
4. That, compared with those for the preceding year, the judicial returns do not present any important variations.

PART I.—CRIMINAL STATISTICS.

Part I. Criminal Statistics. Chapter I. Statistics of Crime.

CHAPTER I.—STATISTICS OF CRIME.

Increase and Decrease of Criminal Offences.—The Criminal offences and charges of all kinds in Ireland, except those determined under the Criminal Law and Procedure (Ireland) Act, 1887, in the years 1887–91,* are given in the following Table for the year 1896, and each year of the preceding decennium.

As regards charges determined summarily the figures indicate the number of persons proceeded against, including those cases in which the charges were dismissed. In the case of Indictable Offences the figures represent the number of crimes committed.

Years	Estimated Population	[illegible] Number	[illegible]	[illegible]	[illegible]	[illegible]	[illegible] Number	[illegible]	[illegible]	[illegible]	[illegible]	[illegible] Number	[illegible]	[illegible]	[illegible]	[illegible]
[illegible]	[illegible]	[illegible]	[illegible]	[illegible]	[illegible]	[illegible]	[illegible]	[illegible]	[illegible]	[illegible]	[illegible]	[illegible]	[illegible]	[illegible]	[illegible]	[illegible]
[illegible]	[illegible]	[illegible]	[illegible]	[illegible]	[illegible]	[illegible]	[illegible]	[illegible]	[illegible]	[illegible]	[illegible]	[illegible]	[illegible]	[illegible]	[illegible]	[illegible]
[illegible]	[illegible]	[illegible]	[illegible]	[illegible]	[illegible]	[illegible]	[illegible]	[illegible]	[illegible]	[illegible]	[illegible]	[illegible]	[illegible]	[illegible]	[illegible]	[illegible]
[illegible]	[illegible]	[illegible]	[illegible]	[illegible]	[illegible]	[illegible]	[illegible]	[illegible]	[illegible]	[illegible]	[illegible]	[illegible]	[illegible]	[illegible]	[illegible]	[illegible]
[illegible]	[illegible]	[illegible]	[illegible]	[illegible]	[illegible]	[illegible]	[illegible]	[illegible]	[illegible]	[illegible]	[illegible]	[illegible]	[illegible]	[illegible]	[illegible]	[illegible]
[illegible]	[illegible]	[illegible]	[illegible]	[illegible]	[illegible]	[illegible]	[illegible]	[illegible]	[illegible]	[illegible]	[illegible]	[illegible]	[illegible]	[illegible]	[illegible]	[illegible]
[illegible]	[illegible]	[illegible]	[illegible]	[illegible]	[illegible]	[illegible]	[illegible]	[illegible]	[illegible]	[illegible]	[illegible]	[illegible]	[illegible]	[illegible]	[illegible]	[illegible]
[illegible]	[illegible]	[illegible]	[illegible]	[illegible]	[illegible]	[illegible]	[illegible]	[illegible]	[illegible]	[illegible]	[illegible]	[illegible]	[illegible]	[illegible]	[illegible]	[illegible]
[illegible]	[illegible]	[illegible]	[illegible]	[illegible]	[illegible]	[illegible]	[illegible]	[illegible]	[illegible]	[illegible]	[illegible]	[illegible]	[illegible]	[illegible]	[illegible]	[illegible]
[illegible]	[illegible]	[illegible]	[illegible]	[illegible]	[illegible]	[illegible]	[illegible]	[illegible]	[illegible]	[illegible]	[illegible]	[illegible]	[illegible]	[illegible]	[illegible]	[illegible]
[illegible]	[illegible]	[illegible]	[illegible]	[illegible]	[illegible]	[illegible]	[illegible]	[illegible]	[illegible]	[illegible]	[illegible]	[illegible]	[illegible]	[illegible]	[illegible]	[illegible]

* [illegible]

† [illegible]

3. Comparison of the Number for last year with the Average Annual Number for the ten years 1884–93 is afforded by the following statement:—

Part I. Criminal Statistics.

Chapter I. Statistics of Crime.

Comparison of crime in 1894 with crime in previous years.

Tables I and 2.

Offences and Charges.	Average 10 years, 1884–93.		Year 1894.		Increase (+) or decrease (—) in 1894 as compared with average.	
	Number.	Rate per 10,000 of estimated population.	Number.	Rate per 10,000 of estimated population.	In Number.	In Rate per 10,000 of population.
Indictable, not disposed of summarily,	6,548	13·4	5,109	11·1	[illegible]	[illegible]
Disposed of summarily,	226,308	472·8	224,616	475·2	[illegible]	[illegible]
Total,	232,856	486·2	229,725	486·3	—3,131	+ 0·1

From these statements it appears that the total number of criminal offences and charges during the year 1894 was 229,725, or 486·3 per 10,000 of the estimated population in the middle of the year, against 228,733, or 481·6 per 10,000 of the estimated population in 1893; and an average of 232,856, or 486·2 per 10,000 of the estimated mean population for the ten years 1884–93; showing an increase of 992 in number, and of 4·7 in the rate per 10,000 persons when compared with the figures for 1893, and a decrease of 3,131 in number, and an increase of 0·1 in the rate per 10,000 persons as compared with the average for the ten years. Offences not disposed of summarily, constituting the more serious group of crimes, are less numerous than in any of the ten years preceding, except 1892, the number for which they slightly exceed, and the absolute number (5,109) of these offences and their ratio to the estimated population (11·1 per 10,000) are considerably below the corresponding averages for the ten years 1884–93. The charges summarily disposed of show a small increase over the number for 1893, and, allowing for the estimated decrease of population, yield a rate slightly over the average for the ten years 1884–93.

Distribution of crime.

General Distribution of Criminal Offences.—The statement on page 18 shows the distribution of criminal offences in Ireland by Provinces, Counties, and large Town Districts, such as the Dublin Metropolitan Police District, the City of Belfast, &c.

From that statement it appears that the 229,725 criminal offences in Ireland in 1894, were distributed as follows throughout the four Provinces:—

Leinster, 82,135, or at the rate of 704·8 per 10,000 of the population; Munster, 69,880, or at the rate of 488·9 per 10,000; Ulster, 57,474, or 358·3 per 10,000; and Connaught, 20,236, or 300·7 per 10,000. Compared with the year 1893, there has been an increase of criminal cases in Leinster to the extent of 3,407, or 4·2 per cent.; a decrease of 1,768, or 2·0 per cent., in Munster; a decrease of 1,319, or 2·3 per cent., in Ulster; and an increase of 572, or 2·7 per cent., in Connaught. The more serious cases (those not determined summarily) have increased slightly in Leinster, where there had been an increase of 6·8 per cent. between 1892 and 1893 and a decline of 11·7 per cent. between 1891 and 1892, and decreased in each of the other provinces, the respective decreases being 15·3 per cent. in Munster, 10·2 per cent. in Ulster, and 6·5 per cent. in Connaught. The less serious offences (those determined summarily) have increased in Leinster and Connaught and decreased in the other two provinces. The increase (4·3 per cent.) in Leinster follows a decrease of 7 per cent. in that province in 1893 as compared with 1892. With reference to the very high rate for the Dublin Metropolitan Police District, it is right to state that the excess is, in great part, due to the fact that the statistics for that district include a large proportion of cases which

(Continued on page 19.)

[illegible]

Counties [illegible]	[illegible]	[illegible]	[illegible]	[illegible]	[illegible]	[illegible]	[illegible]	[illegible]	[illegible]	[illegible]	[illegible]	[illegible]	[illegible]	[illegible]	[illegible]	[illegible]
Total of Ireland	[illegible]	[illegible]	[illegible]	[illegible]	[illegible]	[illegible]	[illegible]	[illegible]	[illegible]	[illegible]	[illegible]	[illegible]	[illegible]	[illegible]	[illegible]	[illegible]
Leinster.																
Carlow	[illegible]	[illegible]	[illegible]	[illegible]	[illegible]	[illegible]	[illegible]	[illegible]	[illegible]	[illegible]	[illegible]	[illegible]	[illegible]	[illegible]	[illegible]	[illegible]
Drogheda Town	[illegible]	[illegible]	[illegible]	[illegible]	[illegible]	[illegible]	[illegible]	[illegible]	[illegible]	[illegible]	[illegible]	[illegible]	[illegible]	[illegible]	[illegible]	[illegible]
Dublin	[illegible]	[illegible]	[illegible]	[illegible]	[illegible]	[illegible]	[illegible]	[illegible]	[illegible]	[illegible]	[illegible]	[illegible]	[illegible]	[illegible]	[illegible]	[illegible]
Dublin Metropolitan Police District	[illegible]	[illegible]	[illegible]	[illegible]	[illegible]	[illegible]	[illegible]	[illegible]	[illegible]	[illegible]	[illegible]	[illegible]	[illegible]	[illegible]	[illegible]	[illegible]
Kildare	[illegible]	[illegible]	[illegible]	[illegible]	[illegible]	[illegible]	[illegible]	[illegible]	[illegible]	[illegible]	[illegible]	[illegible]	[illegible]	[illegible]	[illegible]	[illegible]
Kilkenny	[illegible]	[illegible]	[illegible]	[illegible]	[illegible]	[illegible]	[illegible]	[illegible]	[illegible]	[illegible]	[illegible]	[illegible]	[illegible]	[illegible]	[illegible]	[illegible]
King's County	[illegible]	[illegible]	[illegible]	[illegible]	[illegible]	[illegible]	[illegible]	[illegible]	[illegible]	[illegible]	[illegible]	[illegible]	[illegible]	[illegible]	[illegible]	[illegible]
Longford	[illegible]	[illegible]	[illegible]	[illegible]	[illegible]	[illegible]	[illegible]	[illegible]	[illegible]	[illegible]	[illegible]	[illegible]	[illegible]	[illegible]	[illegible]	[illegible]
Louth	[illegible]	[illegible]	[illegible]	[illegible]	[illegible]	[illegible]	[illegible]	[illegible]	[illegible]	[illegible]	[illegible]	[illegible]	[illegible]	[illegible]	[illegible]	[illegible]
Meath	[illegible]	[illegible]	[illegible]	[illegible]	[illegible]	[illegible]	[illegible]	[illegible]	[illegible]	[illegible]	[illegible]	[illegible]	[illegible]	[illegible]	[illegible]	[illegible]
Queen's County	[illegible]	[illegible]	[illegible]	[illegible]	[illegible]	[illegible]	[illegible]	[illegible]	[illegible]	[illegible]	[illegible]	[illegible]	[illegible]	[illegible]	[illegible]	[illegible]
Westmeath	[illegible]	[illegible]	[illegible]	[illegible]	[illegible]	[illegible]	[illegible]	[illegible]	[illegible]	[illegible]	[illegible]	[illegible]	[illegible]	[illegible]	[illegible]	[illegible]
Wexford	[illegible]	[illegible]	[illegible]	[illegible]	[illegible]	[illegible]	[illegible]	[illegible]	[illegible]	[illegible]	[illegible]	[illegible]	[illegible]	[illegible]	[illegible]	[illegible]
Wicklow	[illegible]	[illegible]	[illegible]	[illegible]	[illegible]	[illegible]	[illegible]	[illegible]	[illegible]	[illegible]	[illegible]	[illegible]	[illegible]	[illegible]	[illegible]	[illegible]
Total of Leinster	[illegible]	[illegible]	[illegible]	[illegible]	[illegible]	[illegible]	[illegible]	[illegible]	[illegible]	[illegible]	[illegible]	[illegible]	[illegible]	[illegible]	[illegible]	[illegible]
Munster.																
Clare	[illegible]	[illegible]	[illegible]	[illegible]	[illegible]	[illegible]	[illegible]	[illegible]	[illegible]	[illegible]	[illegible]	[illegible]	[illegible]	[illegible]	[illegible]	[illegible]
Cork, E.R.	[illegible]	[illegible]	[illegible]	[illegible]	[illegible]	[illegible]	[illegible]	[illegible]	[illegible]	[illegible]	[illegible]	[illegible]	[illegible]	[illegible]	[illegible]	[illegible]
Cork, W.R.	[illegible]	[illegible]	[illegible]	[illegible]	[illegible]	[illegible]	[illegible]	[illegible]	[illegible]	[illegible]	[illegible]	[illegible]	[illegible]	[illegible]	[illegible]	[illegible]
Cork City	[illegible]	[illegible]	[illegible]	[illegible]	[illegible]	[illegible]	[illegible]	[illegible]	[illegible]	[illegible]	[illegible]	[illegible]	[illegible]	[illegible]	[illegible]	[illegible]
Kerry	[illegible]	[illegible]	[illegible]	[illegible]	[illegible]	[illegible]	[illegible]	[illegible]	[illegible]	[illegible]	[illegible]	[illegible]	[illegible]	[illegible]	[illegible]	[illegible]
Limerick	[illegible]	[illegible]	[illegible]	[illegible]	[illegible]	[illegible]	[illegible]	[illegible]	[illegible]	[illegible]	[illegible]	[illegible]	[illegible]	[illegible]	[illegible]	[illegible]
Limerick City	[illegible]	[illegible]	[illegible]	[illegible]	[illegible]	[illegible]	[illegible]	[illegible]	[illegible]	[illegible]	[illegible]	[illegible]	[illegible]	[illegible]	[illegible]	[illegible]
Tipperary, N.R.	[illegible]	[illegible]	[illegible]	[illegible]	[illegible]	[illegible]	[illegible]	[illegible]	[illegible]	[illegible]	[illegible]	[illegible]	[illegible]	[illegible]	[illegible]	[illegible]
Tipperary, S.R.	[illegible]	[illegible]	[illegible]	[illegible]	[illegible]	[illegible]	[illegible]	[illegible]	[illegible]	[illegible]	[illegible]	[illegible]	[illegible]	[illegible]	[illegible]	[illegible]
Waterford	[illegible]	[illegible]	[illegible]	[illegible]	[illegible]	[illegible]	[illegible]	[illegible]	[illegible]	[illegible]	[illegible]	[illegible]	[illegible]	[illegible]	[illegible]	[illegible]
Waterford City	[illegible]	[illegible]	[illegible]	[illegible]	[illegible]	[illegible]	[illegible]	[illegible]	[illegible]	[illegible]	[illegible]	[illegible]	[illegible]	[illegible]	[illegible]	[illegible]
Total of Munster	[illegible]	[illegible]	[illegible]	[illegible]	[illegible]	[illegible]	[illegible]	[illegible]	[illegible]	[illegible]	[illegible]	[illegible]	[illegible]	[illegible]	[illegible]	[illegible]
Ulster.																
Antrim	[illegible]	[illegible]	[illegible]	[illegible]	[illegible]	[illegible]	[illegible]	[illegible]	[illegible]	[illegible]	[illegible]	[illegible]	[illegible]	[illegible]	[illegible]	[illegible]
Armagh	[illegible]	[illegible]	[illegible]	[illegible]	[illegible]	[illegible]	[illegible]	[illegible]	[illegible]	[illegible]	[illegible]	[illegible]	[illegible]	[illegible]	[illegible]	[illegible]
Belfast Town	[illegible]	[illegible]	[illegible]	[illegible]	[illegible]	[illegible]	[illegible]	[illegible]	[illegible]	[illegible]	[illegible]	[illegible]	[illegible]	[illegible]	[illegible]	[illegible]
Carrickfergus Town	[illegible]	[illegible]	[illegible]	[illegible]	[illegible]	[illegible]	[illegible]	[illegible]	[illegible]	[illegible]	[illegible]	[illegible]	[illegible]	[illegible]	[illegible]	[illegible]
Cavan	[illegible]	[illegible]	[illegible]	[illegible]	[illegible]	[illegible]	[illegible]	[illegible]	[illegible]	[illegible]	[illegible]	[illegible]	[illegible]	[illegible]	[illegible]	[illegible]
Donegal	[illegible]	[illegible]	[illegible]	[illegible]	[illegible]	[illegible]	[illegible]	[illegible]	[illegible]	[illegible]	[illegible]	[illegible]	[illegible]	[illegible]	[illegible]	[illegible]
Down	[illegible]	[illegible]	[illegible]	[illegible]	[illegible]	[illegible]	[illegible]	[illegible]	[illegible]	[illegible]	[illegible]	[illegible]	[illegible]	[illegible]	[illegible]	[illegible]
Fermanagh	[illegible]	[illegible]	[illegible]	[illegible]	[illegible]	[illegible]	[illegible]	[illegible]	[illegible]	[illegible]	[illegible]	[illegible]	[illegible]	[illegible]	[illegible]	[illegible]
Londonderry	[illegible]	[illegible]	[illegible]	[illegible]	[illegible]	[illegible]	[illegible]	[illegible]	[illegible]	[illegible]	[illegible]	[illegible]	[illegible]	[illegible]	[illegible]	[illegible]
Monaghan	[illegible]	[illegible]	[illegible]	[illegible]	[illegible]	[illegible]	[illegible]	[illegible]	[illegible]	[illegible]	[illegible]	[illegible]	[illegible]	[illegible]	[illegible]	[illegible]
Tyrone	[illegible]	[illegible]	[illegible]	[illegible]	[illegible]	[illegible]	[illegible]	[illegible]	[illegible]	[illegible]	[illegible]	[illegible]	[illegible]	[illegible]	[illegible]	[illegible]
Total of Ulster	[illegible]	[illegible]	[illegible]	[illegible]	[illegible]	[illegible]	[illegible]	[illegible]	[illegible]	[illegible]	[illegible]	[illegible]	[illegible]	[illegible]	[illegible]	[illegible]
Connaught.																
Galway, E.R.	[illegible]	[illegible]	[illegible]	[illegible]	[illegible]	[illegible]	[illegible]	[illegible]	[illegible]	[illegible]	[illegible]	[illegible]	[illegible]	[illegible]	[illegible]	[illegible]
Galway, W.R.	[illegible]	[illegible]	[illegible]	[illegible]	[illegible]	[illegible]	[illegible]	[illegible]	[illegible]	[illegible]	[illegible]	[illegible]	[illegible]	[illegible]	[illegible]	[illegible]
Galway Town	[illegible]	[illegible]	[illegible]	[illegible]	[illegible]	[illegible]	[illegible]	[illegible]	[illegible]	[illegible]	[illegible]	[illegible]	[illegible]	[illegible]	[illegible]	[illegible]
Leitrim	[illegible]	[illegible]	[illegible]	[illegible]	[illegible]	[illegible]	[illegible]	[illegible]	[illegible]	[illegible]	[illegible]	[illegible]	[illegible]	[illegible]	[illegible]	[illegible]
Mayo	[illegible]	[illegible]	[illegible]	[illegible]	[illegible]	[illegible]	[illegible]	[illegible]	[illegible]	[illegible]	[illegible]	[illegible]	[illegible]	[illegible]	[illegible]	[illegible]
Roscommon	[illegible]	[illegible]	[illegible]	[illegible]	[illegible]	[illegible]	[illegible]	[illegible]	[illegible]	[illegible]	[illegible]	[illegible]	[illegible]	[illegible]	[illegible]	[illegible]
Sligo	[illegible]	[illegible]	[illegible]	[illegible]	[illegible]	[illegible]	[illegible]	[illegible]	[illegible]	[illegible]	[illegible]	[illegible]	[illegible]	[illegible]	[illegible]	[illegible]
Total of Connaught	[illegible]	[illegible]	[illegible]	[illegible]	[illegible]	[illegible]	[illegible]	[illegible]	[illegible]	[illegible]	[illegible]	[illegible]	[illegible]	[illegible]	[illegible]	[illegible]

may be regarded rather as civil transgressions than as criminal offences. Thus, of the 48,741 offences and charges in the district, 11,234 were "offences against Local Acts and Borough By-Laws"; 8,083 were "offences against Public Health Acts"; 2,607 were "offences against Stage and Hackney Carriage Acts," and 4,578 were "offences against Highway Act (including road nuisances)," so that the cases coming under these four headings amount to 24,404, or 50 per cent. of the charges of all kinds in the district, while in the remainder of the country, from whatever cause, such cases form but 9 per cent. of the total number of charges. The preponderance of the cases referred to in Dublin is also shown by the fact that 60 per cent. of the number for the whole country occurred there, although the inhabitants of the district constitute but 8 per cent. of the total population. Part I. Criminal Statistics. — Chapter I. Statistics of Crime. — Distribution of crime.

As regards the high rates for the Cities of Limerick and Waterford, it may be mentioned that 51 per cent. of the total number of charges for the year in the former district, and 48 per cent. of those in the latter come under the head of "Drunkenness and Drunk and Disorderly."

Criminal offences show a decrease in the total **number in 25 counties and districts**, and an increase in 18.

In the following list the counties and districts are arranged in order from that in which there was least crime (in 1894) to that in which there was most:—

1. Wexford.
2. Antrim.
3. Donegal.
4. Down.
5. Sligo.
6. Carrickfergus Town.
7. Roscommon.
8. Fermanagh.
9. Carlow.
10. Leitrim.
11. Monaghan.
12. Mayo.
13. Londonderry.
14. Kilkenny.
15. Meath.
16. **Tyrone.**
17. **Louth.**
18. **Armagh.**
19. **Waterford (County).**
20. **Cavan.**
21. **Cork, W.R.**
22. **Galway, E.R.**
23. **Longford.**
24. **Dublin (County).**
25. **Clare.**
26. **Tipperary, N.R.**
27. **Cork, E.R.**
28. **Wicklow.**
29. **Galway, W.R.**
30. **Limerick (County).**
31. Kerry.
32. Westmeath.
33. King's County.
34. Tipperary, S.R.
35. Queen's County.
36. Belfast City.
37. Kildare.
38. Cork City.
39. Drogheda Town.
40. Galway Town.
41. Limerick City.
42. Waterford City.
43. Dublin Metropolitan Police District.

It will be observed that in the **above list** the seven principal Town Districts occupy most unfavourable positions. Relative position of urban districts.

The tabular statement on page 18 relates to the years 1893 and 1894, but a table is given on page 20 which affords a means of comparison of the number of offences and charges in the several counties, &c., last year, with the average numbers for the ten years preceding. It will be seen from that table that comparing the figures for last year with the average for the ten years, the number of indictable offences in proportion to the population shows an increase in 14 districts, a decrease in 27, and no variation in 2; that the minor offences increased in 27 districts, and decreased in 16; and that taking offences and charges of all kinds, there was an increase in the proportional number in 28 districts, and a decrease in 15. Almost all of the large variations were in the districts having the highest rates, and it will be observed that while, on the one hand, the rate for the Dublin Metropolitan Police District fell from an average of 1,695 per 10,000 of the population to 1,356 per 10,000, being a decrease of nearly 20 per cent., that for Drogheda rose from 618 to 982, being an increase of 59 per cent. Comparison of offences in each county, &c., in 1894, with average numbers for the ten years 1884-93.

Nature of Crimes.

In Police Tables 6 and 7 of the Appendix, the nature of the Crimes committed is set forth in detail. The abstract on page 22 has been constructed from Table 6, which includes the more serious offences, namely, those not dealt with summarily, and gives their distribution throughout Ireland in detail.

Distribution of the more serious offences throughout Ireland. Table 6.

The total number of these cases was 5,100, or at the rate of 10·8 per 10,000 of the population, according to the Census of 1891. Of these, 1,150 or 2·5 per 10,000 of the population, were offences against the person; 371, or 0·8 per 10,000, against property with violence; 2,436, or 5·2 per 10,000, against property without violence; 658, or 1·4 per 10,000, were malicious offences against property. Cases of forgery and offences against the currency were only 36, or 0·1 per 10,000; and all other cases amounted to 456. It will be observed that the rate per 10,000 persons of all offences not disposed of summarily was in Leinster 15·9; Munster, 6·4; Ulster, 4·7; and Connaught, 4·7.

Offences against the person.

In the case of *Offences against the Person* the rates per 10,000 of the population were:—for Leinster 4·4 (including 11·0 in the Dublin Metropolitan District); Munster, 1·9; Ulster, 1·6; Connaught, 1·3. The largest number of these offences, both absolutely and relatively, were committed in the Dublin Metropolitan District, amounting to 386, or 11·0 per 10,000; the next largest, in proportion to population, in the City of Cork, amounting to 5·8 per 10,000. In the King's County, the City of Limerick, and the South Riding of Tipperary the rate was 3·0 per 10,000. In all the other counties and districts the rate was below 3·0 per 10,000, being below 1·0 in four.

Malicious offences against property.

In the case of *Malicious Offences against Property* it appears that the rates per 10,000 of the population were for Leinster 1·3, Munster 2·3, Ulster 0·8, Connaught 1·1: all of them are below the corresponding rates for the year 1893. The highest rate (4·0) was in the County of Clare, where in the year 1893 the rate was 6·4, the next (3·8) in the County of Kerry. No offences of this nature were reported from either Kingstown Town or the Town of Carrickfergus. The lowest rate for any of the remaining districts was 0·2 in the portion of the County of Dublin outside the Metropolitan Police District and in the City of Belfast, and the next lowest 0·3 in the City of Cork.

Forgery and Offences against the currency.

The cases of *Forgery and Offences against the Currency* amounted to the small number of 36, or 0·1 per 10,000 of the population; of these, 18 were in Dublin Metropolitan Police District and 4 in the City of Belfast.

Miscellaneous offences.

Of offences of the *Miscellaneous* class there were 456, or at the rate of 1·0 per 10,000 of the population in 1891. Fifty-seven per cent. of the cases in this group of crimes are made up of the offence of *Intimidation by Threatening Letters, Notices, or otherwise*; the number of cases (261) of this nature is 71 under the number for the preceding year, 82 under that for the year 1892, 92 under that for the year 1891, 103 under the number for 1890, 86 under that for the year 1889, 170 under the number for 1888, and 163 under that for the year 1887; and is far below the numbers (740 and 710 respectively) for the years 1886 and 1885, and also much below the then comparatively low numbers for the two preceding years, when there were but 485 and 335 cases respectively, as compared with 2,851 in 1882, and 5,093 in 1881. With reference to the numbers for the six years, 1887–92, it should be noted that they do not include the charges of Intimidation disposed of under the Criminal Law and Procedure (Ireland) Act, 1887. Of the total number of miscellaneous offences during 1894, shown in Table 6, 148, or 1·3 per 10,000 of the population in 1891, were in Leinster, including 38 cases of intimidation by threatening letters, &c.; 216, or 1·6 per 10,000 inhabitants, were in Munster, including 111 cases of intimidation, of which 80 were in Clare (being 24 under the number for

[illegible]

Counties, Cities, &c.	[illegible]
Total of Ireland,	[illegible]
Leinster.	
Carlow,	[illegible]
Drogheda Town,	[illegible]
Dublin,	[illegible]
Dublin Metropolitan Police District,	[illegible]
Kildare,	[illegible]
Kilkenny,	[illegible]
King's County,	[illegible]
Longford,	[illegible]
Louth,	[illegible]
Meath,	[illegible]
Queen's County,	[illegible]
Westmeath,	[illegible]
Wexford,	[illegible]
Wicklow,	[illegible]
Total of Leinster,	[illegible]
Munster.	
Clare,	[illegible]
Cork, East Riding,	[illegible]
Cork, West Riding,	[illegible]
Cork City,	[illegible]
Kerry,	[illegible]
Limerick,	[illegible]
Limerick City,	[illegible]
Tipperary, North Riding,	[illegible]
Tipperary, South Riding,	[illegible]
Waterford,	[illegible]
Waterford City,	[illegible]
Total of Munster,	[illegible]
Ulster.	
Antrim,	[illegible]
Armagh,	[illegible]
Belfast City,	[illegible]
Carrickfergus Town,	[illegible]
Cavan,	[illegible]
Donegal,	[illegible]
Down,	[illegible]
Fermanagh,	[illegible]
Londonderry,	[illegible]
Monaghan,	[illegible]
Tyrone,	[illegible]
Total of Ulster,	[illegible]
Connaught.	
Galway, East Riding,	[illegible]
Galway, West Riding,	[illegible]
Galway Town,	[illegible]
Leitrim,	[illegible]
Mayo,	[illegible]
Roscommon,	[illegible]
Sligo,	[illegible]
Total of Connaught,	[illegible]

that county in 1893, and 64 more than for 1892; 33 in Kerry (where there were 85 in the preceding year, and 48 in 1892); 24 in the East, and 7 in the West Riding of Cork; and 47 in Limerick County. In Ulster there were 53 miscellaneous offences, or 0·3 per 10,000 of the population in 1891; of these, 19 were cases of intimidation. In Connaught the number of miscellaneous offences was 85, or 1·1 per 10,000 of the population in 1891, including 55 cases of intimidation, of which 29 were in West Galway and 16 in Leitrim.

Part I. Criminal Statistics. Chapter I. Statistics of Crime.

For the indictable offences not disposed of summarily, there were 3,047 persons apprehended, being equal to 60 per cent. of the number of offences as compared with 57 per cent. in the previous year.

Appendix, Table 4.

The following summary showing the rate per 10,000 of the estimated population in the middle of each year represented by the number of cases in each class of serious offences committed in Ireland during last year and each of the ten years preceding, with the average annual rates for those ten years, gives a clear view of the variations which have taken place during the past eleven years in the proportional number of more serious offences in Ireland, allowing for the estimated decrease of the population:—

Offences not determined summarily in 1894 compared with previous years. Table 6.

Classes of Offences.	Number of Offences in every 10,000 of the estimated population											
	Rate										Average for the preceding ten years.	Rate 1894.
	[illegible]	[illegible]	[illegible]	[illegible]	[illegible]	[illegible]	[illegible]	[illegible]	[illegible]	[illegible]		
1. Against the Person,	[illegible]	[illegible]	[illegible]	[illegible]	[illegible]	[illegible]	[illegible]	[illegible]	[illegible]	[illegible]	[illegible]	[illegible]
2. Against Property with Violence,	[illegible]	[illegible]	[illegible]	[illegible]	[illegible]	[illegible]	[illegible]	[illegible]	[illegible]	[illegible]	[illegible]	[illegible]
3. Against Property without Violence,	[illegible]	[illegible]	[illegible]	[illegible]	[illegible]	[illegible]	[illegible]	[illegible]	[illegible]	[illegible]	[illegible]	[illegible]
4. Malicious Offences against Property,	[illegible]	[illegible]	[illegible]	[illegible]	[illegible]	[illegible]	[illegible]	[illegible]	[illegible]	[illegible]	[illegible]	[illegible]
5. Forgery and Offences against the Currency,	[illegible]	[illegible]	[illegible]	[illegible]	[illegible]	[illegible]	[illegible]	[illegible]	[illegible]	[illegible]	[illegible]	[illegible]
6. Not included in foregoing,	[illegible]	[illegible]	[illegible]	[illegible]	[illegible]	[illegible]	[illegible]	[illegible]	[illegible]	[illegible]	[illegible]	[illegible]
Total,	[illegible]	[illegible]	[illegible]	[illegible]	[illegible]	[illegible]	[illegible]	[illegible]	[illegible]	[illegible]	[illegible]	[illegible]

This statement shows that in 1894 the number of serious crimes in proportion to the estimated population was considerably below the average for the preceding ten years, and that there was a decrease in each class of such crimes, except offences against property with violence, in which there was a slight increase.

Compared with the year 1893, there was a slight decrease in the total rate, increases in two of the classes being more than counterbalanced by decreases in the remaining four.

A more minute consideration of Table 6 in the Appendix will show that there were 22 cases of murders of infants, of which 5 were in Leinster, 6 in Munster, 7 in Ulster, and 4 in Connaught. In the case of other murders there were 17 in Ireland in 1894, as compared with 20 in 1893, 30 in 1892, 28 in 1891, 20 in 1890, 38 in 1889, 36 in 1888, 29 in 1887, 35 in 1886, 18 in 1885, and 21 in 1884. Of these 17 murders, 8 were in Leinster, 5 in Munster, 3 in Ulster, and 1 in Connaught. There was 1 each in Longford, Meath, Cork East Riding, Kerry, Tipperary North Riding, Antrim, Cavan, Down, and Roscommon; and 2 in Carlow County, Dublin Metropolitan Police District, Kildare County, and Cork City, respectively. There were not any such murders in Drogheda Town, Dublin County, Kilkenny, King's County, Louth, Queen's County, Westmeath, Wexford, or Wicklow, in the Province of Leinster; nor in Clare, Cork West Riding, Limerick County, Limerick City, Tipperary South Riding, Waterford County, or the City of Waterford, in the Province of Munster; nor in Armagh, Belfast City, Carrickfergus Town, Donegal, Fermanagh, Londonderry, Monaghan, or Tyrone, in the Province of Ulster; nor in Galway East Riding, Galway West Riding, Galway Town, Leitrim, Mayo, or Sligo, in the Province of Connaught. There were 9 attempts to murder in 1894, as compared with 8 in 1893, 9 in 1892, 8 in 1891, 10 in 1890, 9 in 1889, 9 in 1888, 7 in 1887, 12 in 1886, 5 in 1885, and 1 in 1884. There were 26 cases of shooting at,

Murders, attempts to murder, shooting at, wounding, &c.

[illegible] wounding, stabbing, &c., with intent to do bodily harm in 1894, compared with 130 in 1893, 101 in 1892, 105 in 1891, 131 in 1890, 114 in 1889, 118 in 1888, 151 in 1887, 148 in 1886, 145 in 1885, and 152 in 1884. The cases of assault and inflicting bodily harm were 443 compared with 436 in 1893, 416 in 1892, 473 in 1891, 498 in 1890, 566 in 1889, 560 in 1888, 610 in 1887, 720 in 1886, 642 in 1885, and 697 in 1884. The number of *offences against property with violence* was 374, being 15 under the number for the preceding year, and 11 over the average for the ten years 1884–93.

Offences against property without violence.

Offences against property without violence, which, after having declined from 2,876 in 1887, 3,183 in 1886, and an average of 2,796 for the seven years 1879–85, to 2,803 in 1888, rose to 2,970 in 1889, fell to 2,412 in 1890, rose again in 1891 to 2,617, fell to 2,393 in 1892, and rose to 2,392 in 1893 and to 2,435 last year. As usual, cases of simple larceny form the great bulk of the crime in this class. It is also again to be noted that a very large proportion of this class of crime is committed in the Dublin Metropolitan Police District. Of the 2,435 offences against property without violence in Ireland, included in Table 6, no less than 1,881, or 77 per cent. were in that District, and of the 1,468 simple larceny cases, 1,274 occurred there.

The classes of *malicious offences against property*, *offences against the currency*, and *miscellaneous offences*, included in Table 6, have already been sufficiently dealt with in the general comments on crime not determined summarily.

Offences disposed of summarily. Table 7.

In Table 7 of the Appendix details are given of the cases determined summarily, which include those usually dealt with in police courts.

These, as previously shown, amount to a total of 218,626, and constitute 98 per cent. of the total number of criminal offences. It is also in this class that the preponderance of town over rural crime is specially noticeable.

Among the offences disposed of summarily last year the more important are set out in the following Statement, and a comparison instituted with each of the ten years preceding.

[illegible]	[illegible]	[illegible]	[illegible]	[illegible]	[illegible]	[illegible]	[illegible]	[illegible]	[illegible]	[illegible]	Average of Ten Years 1884–93	[illegible]
Common Assaults,	[illegible]	[illegible]	[illegible]	[illegible]	[illegible]	[illegible]	[illegible]	[illegible]	[illegible]	[illegible]	[illegible]	[illegible]
Drunkenness, and Drunk and Disorderly,	[illegible]	[illegible]	[illegible]	[illegible]	[illegible]	[illegible]	[illegible]	[illegible]	[illegible]	[illegible]	[illegible]	[illegible]

Compared with the numbers for the year 1893 there has been a decrease of 3,068, or 12·5 per cent. in common assaults, and a decrease of 1,350, or 1·5 per cent. in cases of drunkenness and disorderly conduct in connexion therewith, the decrease in the latter class of offences following a decrease of 3,482, or 3·9 per cent. between 1892 and 1893, and a decrease of 7,831, or 7·3 per cent. in 1892, as compared with 1891, and the decrease in Common Assaults following an increase of 1,297, or 5·5 per cent. between 1892 and 1893. The "Common Assaults" for last year were equal to an annual rate of 48 per 10,000 of the estimated population against an average rate of 55 per 10,000 for the ten years 1884–93, and the cases coming under "Drunkenness and Drunk and Disorderly" were equivalent to 188 for every 10,000 persons against an average rate of 188 per 10,000; this rate reaching 320 per 10,000 of the (1891) population in the Dublin Metropolitan Police District, 807 in the City of Limerick, and 789 in the City of Waterford. As these cases constitute about one half of all the cases dealt with in the Police and Petty Sessions courts, are closely connected with one another, and are the starting points of many other criminal actions, their import is very great when reviewing the general condition of the criminal classes.

Habitual Drunkards. Table 11.

In connexion with the statistics of drunkenness, a return of habitual drunkards (Table 11, page 84) has been compiled; it gives the number of persons convicted three cases or upwards of being "Drunk" or "Drunk and Disorderly" in 1894 (so far as known to the Police).

Part I. Criminal Statistics.

Chapter I. Statistics of Crime.

Habitual Drunkards. Table 11.

The chief value of the habitual drunkenness return is in the light it throws upon the amount of town crime, which has been noticed as excessive. Taking the seven police jurisdictions outside Dublin, of Belfast, Cork, Limerick, Waterford, Galway, Drogheda, and Carrickfergus, with (in 1891) an aggregate population of 427,[illegible], the habitual drunkards were 712, or 16·4 per 10,000 of the population. In the rest of Ireland, outside the Metropolitan district, with a population of 3,926,000, the number was only 2,108, or 5·4 in the 10,000. In the Dublin Metropolitan Police District, with a population of 352,000, the number was 123, or 3·5 per 10,000 population. Compared with 1893 there was a decrease in the number in Dublin, Cork, Waterford, and Belfast, but an increase in each of the other town jurisdictions. In the rest of Ireland there was a decrease, from 2,362 to 2,108. In all Ireland, there was a decrease of [illegible], viz., from 3,2[illegible] to 2,987. Of this total, 2,306 were convicted three times and less than five times, 546 five times and less than ten times, and 35 ten times and upwards.

Illegally selling intoxicating Drinks. Table 7.

It will be observed from Table 7 that the number of cases of "Illegally selling intoxicating drinks," which had fallen from 3,783 in 1892, to 3,308 in 1893, further declined last year to 2,293.

Cruelty to animals. Local Acts and Borough Bye-laws. Public Health and Nuisances Removal Acts. Unlawful possession of stolen goods. Highway Act.

Cases of cruelty to animals were 2,268 in 1893, and 2,392 in 1894. *Offences against Local Acts and Borough Bye-laws* show an increase, from 10,986 in 1893, to 13,738 in 1894, following a decrease of 216 in 1893: the 13,738 cases for last year include 9,594 cases in the Dublin Metropolitan Police district. The number of *offences against the Public Health and Nuisances Removal Acts* was 8,862, or 56 more than in 1893: of the 8,862 charges under these Acts, 3,085 were in the Dublin Metropolitan district. In a considerable number of districts no offences against these Acts were recorded. Cases of unlawful possession of stolen goods fell from 1,041 in 1893, to 910 last year, and of the latter number, 870 were in the Dublin Metropolitan Police District. The offences against the *Highway Act*, including Nuisances on Public Roads, after having fallen from 14,867 in 1892, to 11,924 in 1893, rose last year to 13,633. The other statistics given in Table 7 do not call for any special remark, but, nevertheless, contain many items of considerable interest.

Criminal Law and Procedure (Ireland) Act, 1887.

There were not any cases under the Criminal Law and Procedure (Ireland) Act, 1887, during the year.

CHAPTER II.—MODES OF PROCEDURE FOR PUNISHING CRIME.

Chapter II. *Procedure.*

The Police act as public prosecutors in the great majority of cases in Ireland. In minor cases they undertake the sole duty of prosecuting, and in most of the more serious offences the preliminary proceedings are instituted by them. In all the counties of Ireland, except the County and City of Dublin, the Cities of Cork, Limerick, and Waterford, and the Counties of Carlow, Cavan, Down, Galway, Kildare, Limerick, Longford, Mayo, Monaghan, Queen's County, Roscommon, Waterford, and Westmeath, there are two Crown Solicitors, one of whom deals with cases at Quarter Sessions, the other with the more serious cases which come before the Judges at Assizes.

Coroners' Courts still deal with cases where criminal offences are involved, and Coroners' Juries frequently find verdicts implicating or exonerating certain persons in cases of homicide, &c. It is not, however, the custom now to bring prisoners charged with

Part I. Criminal Statistics. Chapter II. Procedure.

homicide, &c., before Coroners' Courts, and in a large number of cases the finding of the Jury relates merely to the cause of death.

A special feature in the administration of Criminal Law in Ireland is the proclamation of certain Districts under special Acts of Parliament. The following is a general statement relating to these Special Acts and the extent of their application in Ireland at the close of the past year.

Districts proclaimed under special Acts. Tables 13, 15, 16.

Under the Act 6 Wm. IV., chap. 13, the following counties were proclaimed as requiring additional Police at the end of 1894:—Clare, Cork, Galway, Kerry, and Limerick.

Under the Peace Preservation (Ireland) Act, 1881, as continued and amended by the Peace Preservation (Ireland) Continuance Act, 1886, the Criminal Law and Procedure (Ireland) Act, 1887, and the Expiring Laws Continuance Acts, two provinces, viz., Munster and Connaught; all of the province of Leinster except the Counties of Louth and Wicklow and the City of Kilkenny; and the City of Belfast, the City of Londonderry, and parts of the Counties of Armagh, Donegal, and Monaghan were, at the end of 1894, under the operation of Proclamations in Council prohibiting the carrying or having of arms, &c. In Ulster the prohibition against carrying arms included the Counties of Cavan, Fermanagh, and Monaghan, one Barony in Down, and five Baronies in Tyrone.

No part of the country was subject to Proclamations nor to Orders in Council under the Criminal Law and Procedure (Ireland) Act, 1887, during any portion of the year 1894.

Results of preliminary inquiry as to offences. Table 4.

Of 3,066 persons apprehended in 1894 for offences punishable after indictment and trial by jury, 978, or 31·9 per cent. were discharged; 107, or 3·5 per cent. were bailed or committed in default of finding bail pending further examination; and 1,906, or 62·6 per cent. were committed for trial or admitted to bail pending trial.

Disposal of bills of indictment by grand jury. Table 21.

The result of proceedings at Assizes, Commissions, and Quarter Sessions in 1894, regarding 346 persons committed for trial, was that in 101 cases no bill was found by the Grand Jury, in 123 cases no prosecution took place, and in 67 bail was accepted and the cases not tried. In addition to those bailed and not tried, or where there was no prosecution, there were 48 cases in which trials were postponed.

Disposal of persons tried by jury. Table 32.

Of 2,004 persons tried by jury in 1894, 528, or 26·3 per cent. were acquitted; besides 13, or 0·6 per cent. who were found insane or acquitted on the ground of insanity; 1,463, or 73·0 per cent. were convicted.

A summary of the number of prosecutions at Assizes on Circuit during the year ended 31st March, 1894, in respect of which expenses were incurred, is given at page 60, and other details regarding the subject will be found in Table 28, pp. 94–5.

The following statement shows for 1894, and each of the ten years preceding, the number of persons tried by jury at Assizes, at the Dublin Commission Court and at Quarter Sessions, and how their cases were disposed of:—

Years	Tried	Convicted or Detained as Insane	Acquitted	Proportion per cent. of those Tried who were — Convicted or Detained as Insane	Acquitted
1884,	2,193	1,584	608	72·1	26·1
1885,	2,155	1,383	673	73·6	26·4
1886,	2,314	1,658	679	70·7	29·3
1887,	2,091	1,534	557	73·0	28·0
1888,	1,904	1,440	464	75·6	24·4
1889,	1,856	1,343	513	72·4	27·6
1890,	1,997	1,557	440	78·0	22·0
1891,	1,932	1,365	567	73·0	29·3
1892,	1,858	1,360	498	73·2	26·8
1893,	1,819	1,330	489	73·1	26·9
1894,	2,004	1,463	528	73·0	26·3

In the next statement the sentences inflicted on persons convicted, after trial by jury, in 1894, are set out in comparison with similar cases in 1893:—

Part I. General Statistics. Chapter II. Procedure. Disposal of men and boys, women and girls, committed for trial, and persons convicted, 1893–94.

Results of Persons Charged for Trial by Jury.

How Disposed of.	1894. Total.	Men and Boys.	Women and Girls.	Previously Convicted. Men and Boys.	Previously Convicted. Women and Girls.	1893. Total.	Men and Boys.	Women and Girls.	Previously Convicted. Men and Boys.	Previously Convicted. Women and Girls.
[illegible]	[illegible]	[illegible]	[illegible]	[illegible]	[illegible]	[illegible]	[illegible]	[illegible]	[illegible]	[illegible]
[illegible]	[illegible]	[illegible]	[illegible]	[illegible]	[illegible]	[illegible]	[illegible]	[illegible]	[illegible]	[illegible]
[illegible]	[illegible]	[illegible]	[illegible]	[illegible]	[illegible]	[illegible]	[illegible]	[illegible]	[illegible]	[illegible]
[illegible]	[illegible]	[illegible]	[illegible]	[illegible]	[illegible]	[illegible]	[illegible]	[illegible]	[illegible]	[illegible]
[illegible]	[illegible]	[illegible]	[illegible]	[illegible]	[illegible]	[illegible]	[illegible]	[illegible]	[illegible]	[illegible]
[illegible]	[illegible]	[illegible]	[illegible]	[illegible]	[illegible]	[illegible]	[illegible]	[illegible]	[illegible]	[illegible]
[illegible]	[illegible]	[illegible]	[illegible]	[illegible]	[illegible]	[illegible]	[illegible]	[illegible]	[illegible]	[illegible]
[illegible]	[illegible]	[illegible]	[illegible]	[illegible]	[illegible]	[illegible]	[illegible]	[illegible]	[illegible]	[illegible]
Sentenced to death	[illegible]	[illegible]	[illegible]	[illegible]	[illegible]	[illegible]	[illegible]	[illegible]	[illegible]	[illegible]
Penal servitude:										
[illegible]	[illegible]	[illegible]	[illegible]	[illegible]	[illegible]	[illegible]	[illegible]	[illegible]	[illegible]	[illegible]
[illegible]	[illegible]	[illegible]	[illegible]	[illegible]	[illegible]	[illegible]	[illegible]	[illegible]	[illegible]	[illegible]
[illegible]	[illegible]	[illegible]	[illegible]	[illegible]	[illegible]	[illegible]	[illegible]	[illegible]	[illegible]	[illegible]
[illegible]	[illegible]	[illegible]	[illegible]	[illegible]	[illegible]	[illegible]	[illegible]	[illegible]	[illegible]	[illegible]
[illegible]	[illegible]	[illegible]	[illegible]	[illegible]	[illegible]	[illegible]	[illegible]	[illegible]	[illegible]	[illegible]
[illegible]										
[illegible]	[illegible]	[illegible]	[illegible]	[illegible]	[illegible]	[illegible]	[illegible]	[illegible]	[illegible]	[illegible]
[illegible]	[illegible]	[illegible]	[illegible]	[illegible]	[illegible]	[illegible]	[illegible]	[illegible]	[illegible]	[illegible]
[illegible]	[illegible]	[illegible]	[illegible]	[illegible]	[illegible]	[illegible]	[illegible]	[illegible]	[illegible]	[illegible]
[illegible]	[illegible]	[illegible]	[illegible]	[illegible]	[illegible]	[illegible]	[illegible]	[illegible]	[illegible]	[illegible]
[illegible]	[illegible]	[illegible]	[illegible]	[illegible]	[illegible]	[illegible]	[illegible]	[illegible]	[illegible]	[illegible]
[illegible]	[illegible]	[illegible]	[illegible]	[illegible]	[illegible]	[illegible]	[illegible]	[illegible]	[illegible]	[illegible]

From this it appears that, exclusive of those detained as insane, 1,486 persons were convicted for serious offences in 1894, as compared with 1,396 in 1893, showing an increase of 91, following an increase of 19 in 1893, as compared with 1892. Of the number in 1894, 1,283 were males, and 203 females. In 1893, the respective numbers were 1,193 males, and 200 females. Of the persons convicted, two (both males) were sentenced to death; 76 (71 males and 5 females) were sentenced to penal servitude, 6 for over 10 years, 27 for above 5 and up to 10 years, and 43 for 5 years; 1,067 (919 males and 148 females) were sentenced to various terms of imprisonment. Nine [illegible] (all males) were sent to Reformatory Schools.

The following statement shows the results of proceedings for the punishment of crime dealt with summarily in 1894, as compared with 1893, distinguishing the sexes:—

Part II. Criminal Statistics. Chapter II. Persons. Proceedings for offences determined summarily. Number of men and boys compared with those of women and girls. Table 9.

PERSONS PROCEEDED AGAINST SUMMARILY.

How Disposed of.	Total, 1894.	1894. Men and Boys.	1894. Women and Girls.	1894. Proportion per Cent. Men and Boys.	1894. Proportion per Cent. Women and Girls.	Total, 1893.	1893. Men and Boys.	1893. Women and Girls.	1893. Proportion per Cent. Men and Boys.	1893. Proportion per Cent. Women and Girls.
Total Number proceeded against,	[illegible]	[illegible]	[illegible]	[illegible]	[illegible]	[illegible]	[illegible]	[illegible]	[illegible]	[illegible]
Discharged	[illegible]	[illegible]	[illegible]	[illegible]	[illegible]	[illegible]	[illegible]	[illegible]	[illegible]	[illegible]
Total Convicted	[illegible]	[illegible]	[illegible]	[illegible]	[illegible]	[illegible]	[illegible]	[illegible]	[illegible]	[illegible]
Unclassed Punishments,	[illegible]	[illegible]	[illegible]	[illegible]	[illegible]	[illegible]	[illegible]	[illegible]	[illegible]	[illegible]
Classed Punishments,	[illegible]	[illegible]	[illegible]	[illegible]	[illegible]	[illegible]	[illegible]	[illegible]	[illegible]	[illegible]
Number not Committed, viz.:— Total	[illegible]	[illegible]	[illegible]	[illegible]	[illegible]	[illegible]	[illegible]	[illegible]	[illegible]	[illegible]
Fined,	[illegible]	[illegible]	[illegible]	[illegible]	[illegible]	[illegible]	[illegible]	[illegible]	[illegible]	[illegible]
To find Sureties or Recognizances,	[illegible]	[illegible]	[illegible]	[illegible]	[illegible]	[illegible]	[illegible]	[illegible]	[illegible]	[illegible]
Delivered to Army or Navy,	[illegible]	[illegible]	[illegible]	[illegible]	[illegible]	[illegible]	[illegible]	[illegible]	[illegible]	[illegible]
Whipped,	[illegible]	[illegible]	[illegible]	[illegible]	[illegible]	[illegible]	[illegible]	[illegible]	[illegible]	[illegible]
Number Committed, viz.:— Total	[illegible]	[illegible]	[illegible]	[illegible]	[illegible]	[illegible]	[illegible]	[illegible]	[illegible]	[illegible]
To Prison, 14 days or under,	[illegible]	[illegible]	[illegible]	[illegible]	[illegible]	[illegible]	[illegible]	[illegible]	[illegible]	[illegible]
1 month and above 14 days,	[illegible]	[illegible]	[illegible]	[illegible]	[illegible]	[illegible]	[illegible]	[illegible]	[illegible]	[illegible]
2 months and above 1 month,	[illegible]	[illegible]	[illegible]	[illegible]	[illegible]	[illegible]	[illegible]	[illegible]	[illegible]	[illegible]
3 months and above 2 months,	[illegible]	[illegible]	[illegible]	[illegible]	[illegible]	[illegible]	[illegible]	[illegible]	[illegible]	[illegible]
6 months and above 3 months,	[illegible]	[illegible]	[illegible]	[illegible]	[illegible]	[illegible]	[illegible]	[illegible]	[illegible]	[illegible]
Above 6 months,	[illegible]	[illegible]	[illegible]	[illegible]	[illegible]	[illegible]	[illegible]	[illegible]	[illegible]	[illegible]
To Reformatory Schools,	[illegible]	[illegible]	[illegible]	[illegible]	[illegible]	[illegible]	[illegible]	[illegible]	[illegible]	[illegible]
To Industrial Schools,	[illegible]	[illegible]	[illegible]	[illegible]	[illegible]	[illegible]	[illegible]	[illegible]	[illegible]	[illegible]

Of the 218,025 persons proceeded against summarily in 1894, there were 31,[illegible] discharged, and 187,102 convicted, as compared with 32,810 and 186,[illegible] respectively in 1893. Of those convicted in 1894, 157,830 were males and 29,272 females. Of unclassed punishments there were 20,814 (15,775 males and 5,039 females). Of classed punishments there were 166,288 (142,045 males and 24,243 females). Of 150,[illegible] persons not committed, 148,607 (136,956 males and 11,651 females), or 79·3 per cent. of the total number convicted, were fined; 3,485 (2,449 males and 1,036 females) were required to find sureties or recognizances; 310 were given up to the military or naval authorities, and 10 were whipped. Of the persons committed, 4,287 (3,106 males and 1,181 females) were committed to prison for 14 days or under; 5,018 (3,579 males and 1,439 females) for one month and above 14 days; 2,338 (2,094 males and 244 females) for 2 months and over 1 month; 755 (552 males and 203 females) for 3 months and above 2 months; 299 (252 males and 47 females) for 6 months and above 3 months, and 28 (24 males and 4 females) for above 6 months. There were 110 young persons (100 males and 10 females) sent to Reformatory Schools, and 283 (217 males and 66 females) sent to Industrial Schools.

Court for consideration of Crown Cases.

In the Court for the consideration of Crown Cases Reserved, constituted under 11 & 12 Vic., cap. 78, there were 2 cases before the Court in 1894; in both cases the conviction was affirmed.

351

CHAPTER III.—CRIMINALS AND OTHERS IN CONFINEMENT, AND KNOWN CRIMINALS AT LARGE.

Part I. Criminal Statistics.

Chapter III. Criminals, &c., in Confinement, and at large.

The statistics of persons in confinement, with a view to punishment for or prevention of crime, include actual criminals, persons accused of criminal offences, debtors, children detained in industrial and reformatory schools, and criminal and dangerous lunatics.

In the following statement the number of prisoners, &c., admitted to various places of confinement during the year 1884 is set out:—

Admissions to different places of detention compared.

Admissions to Places of Detention.	Men and Boys.	Women and Girls.	Total.	Per cent.
Total in all Ireland,	24,9[illegible]	13,[illegible]72	38,[illegible]80	100
Into Larger Local Prisons,*	21,395	10,886	32,[illegible]81	83·4
Into Bridewells,	1,308	309	1,617	4·1
Into Lock-ups,	61	18	59	0·2
Into Minor Local Prisons,	1,302	437	1,739	4·4
Into Lunatic Asylums (as criminals or dangerous),	1,475	1,142	2,617	6·6
Into Industrial Schools,	604	476	1,[illegible]	[illegible]
Into Reformatory Schools,	130	13	143	0·3

* Including ordinary prisoners only.

It would thus appear that there were 39,58[illegible] persons admitted to places of confinement during the year, but this number is somewhat in excess of the fact, as children sent to Reformatories and some lunatics were confined in Local Prisons prior to their final disposal in schools and lunatic asylums. It must also be noticed that some of the prisoners confined in prison during the year were committed more than once during the period.

The distribution of persons under detention, at the end of the year 1884, among the different kinds of places of confinement, is shown in the following statement:—

Persons detained in each class compared.

Classification of Persons Detained at end of Year.	Men and Boys.	Women and Girls.	Total.	Per cent.
Total in all Ireland,	13,409	9,[illegible]	22,[illegible]	100·0
Ordinary Criminals in Larger Local Prisons,	1,875	614	2,[illegible]	11·0
In Bridewells,	13		13	0·1
In Lock-ups,	–	–	–	–
In Minor Local Prisons,	29	2	31	0·1
Criminals confined in Civil Hospitals, and First Class Misdemeanants,	5	2	7	–
Convicts,	427	37	464	2·0
Military or Naval Prisoners,	108	4	112	0·5
In Lunatic Asylums (as criminals or dangerous),	5,267	3,434	8,701	[illegible]
In Reformatories,	925	218	1,143	[illegible]
In Industrial Schools,	[illegible]	[illegible]	7,[illegible]*	[illegible]

* Not including those in Schools, [illegible]

It appears from this statement that at the close of the year 1884, there were [illegible] persons detained in places of confinement, either for the punishment or the prevention

PART I. CRIMINAL STATISTICS. Committals, Convictions, &c., for Offences, and Condition of Prisons.

of crime. Among the 20,4[illegible] there were 7,8[illegible] children in Industrial schools and 8,801 [illegible], making a total of 16,814, or more than four-fifths of the entire number, who (with a few exceptions) were not actual criminals, but were detained as a preventive measure.

Prisons.

The Prisons of Ireland consist of five classes, namely:—1st, Three Convict Prisons; 2nd, Larger Local Prisons, of which there were 20 at the close of the year 1894; 3rd, Minor Local Prisons, 8 in number, at the same date; 4th, Bridewells, which numbered 16; and "Lockups" of which there was one. Tables 15 to 19, pp. 56–9, give various particulars as to the inmates of these institutions.

The number of commitments of ordinary criminals to larger local prisons in the year 1894, compared with 1893, was as follows:—

—	1894.	1893.	Increase in 1894.	Decrease in 1894.
Men and Boys,	21,711	22,408	–	698
Women and Girls,	11,384	10,924	–	790
Total,	33,094	34,582	–	1,488

There was a decrease of 698, or 3·1 per cent., in the number of males committed as compared with the number for 1893, and a decrease of 790, or 6·9 per cent., in the number of females; the decrease for both sexes being 1,488, following an increase of 354 males and a decrease of 406 females in 1893, as compared with 1892, and a decrease of 4,269 persons (1,936 males and 2,333 females) between 1891 and 1892.

Degree of education of prisoners. Table 15(a).

The state of education of those committed in 1894 is given in the following summary by sexes:—

Degree of Instruction.	Total of both Sexes.	Men and Boys.	Women and Girls.	Proportion per cent.	
				Males.	Females.
Total,	33,093	21,913	10,684	100·	100·
Read and write well,	13,346	10,093	4,433	55·[illegible]	[illegible]
Neither read nor write,	9,362	3,894	4,217	[illegible]	[illegible]
Read, or read and write imperfectly,	8,802	4,263	1,103	[illegible]	[illegible]
Superior instruction,	383	319	10	1·5	[illegible]
Instruction not ascertained,	1	1	–	–	–

From the following statement it appears that of 31,607 commitments to larger district prisons of ordinary criminals during last year, 22,749, or 72 per cent., were recommitments. The proportion of recommitments in the case of females is 86 per cent. of the total of that sex, while in the case of males it is only 65 per cent., showing, as in former years, a greater proportion of habitual criminals among female than among male prisoners :—

PART I. CRIMINAL STATISTICS. — CHAPTER III. Criminals, &c., in Confinement and at large. — Recommitments of ordinary criminals. Table 16 (a).

COMMITMENTS OF ORDINARY CRIMINALS.

	1883.	1884.				
		Number.			Percentage.	
	Total.	Total.	Male.	Female.	Male.	Female.
Total commitments,	[illegible]	31,607	[illegible]	[illegible]	100·	100·
First commitments,	[illegible]	[illegible]	[illegible]	[illegible]	35	14
Recommitments,	[illegible]	22,749	[illegible]	[illegible]	65	86

A more detailed statement is here given as to the number of recommitments of those criminals committed more than once.

Number of times those recommitted were previously committed.	Total of both Sexes.	Men.	Women.	Proportion per cent.		
				Total of both Sexes.	Men.	Women.
Total number of recommitments,	22,749	[illegible]	[illegible]	100·	100·	100·
Once previously,	[illegible]	[illegible]	[illegible]	17·3	[illegible]	9·6
Twice do.,	2,301	[illegible]	[illegible]	10·1	[illegible]	7·3
Thrice do.,	[illegible]	[illegible]	[illegible]	7·4	[illegible]	6·1
Four times previously,	1,250	[illegible]	[illegible]	5·5	[illegible]	4·7
Five times do.,	1,040	[illegible]	[illegible]	4·6	[illegible]	3·6
Six or seven times previously,	[illegible]	[illegible]	[illegible]	7·1	[illegible]	5·9
Eight, nine, or ten times do.,	1,687	[illegible]	[illegible]	7·4	[illegible]	7·1
Above ten times,	9,233	[illegible]	[illegible]	40·6	30·7	55·4

From this it appears that of the 22,749 prisoners who were committed more than once, [illegible], or 17·3 per cent., had been previously committed once; 2,301, or 10·1 per cent., twice; [illegible], or 7·4 per cent., three times; 1,250, or 5·5 per cent., four times; 1,040, or 4·6 per cent., five times; [illegible], or 7·1 per cent., six or seven times; 1,687, or 7·4 per cent., eight, nine, or ten times; and 9,233, or 40·6 per cent., above ten times. The percentage of females previously committed above ten times was 55·4 as compared with 30·7 among

The following summary shows, by sexes, the age of the ordinary prisoners (other than debtors and persons charged with military and naval offences) committed to the Larger Local Prisons in Ireland in 1894, together with the proportions per cent. at the several age periods:—

Ages.	Total of both Sexes.	Men and Boys.	Women and Girls.	Proportion per cent.	
				Men and Boys.	Women and Girls.
Total,	[illegible]	[illegible]	[illegible]	100	100
Under twelve years,	56	56	[illegible]	[illegible]	[illegible]
Twelve years and under sixteen,	[illegible]	[illegible]	83	[illegible]	[illegible]
Sixteen years and under twenty-one,	[illegible]	[illegible]	[illegible]	[illegible]	[illegible]
Twenty-one years and under thirty,	[illegible]	[illegible]	[illegible]	[illegible]	[illegible]
Thirty years and under forty,	[illegible]	[illegible]	[illegible]	[illegible]	[illegible]
Forty years and under fifty,	[illegible]	[illegible]	[illegible]	[illegible]	[illegible]
Fifty years and under sixty,	[illegible]	[illegible]	[illegible]	[illegible]	[illegible]
Sixty years and upwards,	[illegible]	[illegible]	[illegible]	[illegible]	[illegible]
Age not ascertained,	3	3	—	—	—

Occupations of ordinary prisoners. Table 13 (c). The statistics of the occupations of ordinary prisoners committed during the year 1894, are given in Table 13 (c), page 87. They show the usual large proportion of prostitutes and unoccupied women of bad character, the numbers under these heads being [illegible] and [illegible] respectively, out of a total of [illegible] female prisoners.

CRIMINAL AND DANGEROUS LUNATICS.

Criminal and Dangerous Lunatics in Asylums. Table 23. The following summary shows the number of criminal lunatics and dangerous lunatics charged with intent to commit crime detained in lunatic asylums, the authority under which they were committed, and the mode of their disposal during the year:—

Criminal Lunatics and Dangerous Lunatics charged with Intent to commit Crime.	Year ended [illegible]		
	Men.	Women.	Total.
Total number of such lunatics under detention during year,	[illegible]	[illegible]	[illegible]
Under detention at commencement of year,	[illegible]	[illegible]	[illegible]
Committed by Justices, under 30 & 31 Vic., c. 118,	[illegible]	[illegible]	[illegible]
Received from Prisons under warrant of Lord Lieutenant,	[illegible]	[illegible]	[illegible]
Received from other Asylums,	2	—	2
Received under warrant of the Secretary of State for War,	10	—	10
Total number disposed of during year,	[illegible]	[illegible]	[illegible]
Discharged as recovering, &c., on certificate of Resident Medical Superintendent,	615	[illegible]	[illegible]
Died,	406	[illegible]	[illegible]
Given to their friends,	[illegible]	[illegible]	[illegible]
Became ordinary patients on expiration of sentence,	[illegible]	16	[illegible]

The following summary shows the judgments or orders under which criminal and dangerous lunatics were committed to asylums in Ireland in 1894:—

Part II.
Criminal Statistics.
Criminal Lunatics, Dangerous Lunatics, &c.
Criminal and dangerous lunatics. Judgments or orders of committal.

Judgments or Orders of Committal.	Males.	Females.	Total of both Sexes.	Proportion per cent.
Total committed during year,	1,478	1,082	2,560	100·0
Committed to asylums by Justices as dangerous, under sec. 10 of 30 & 31 Vic., c. 118, & 10,	1,380	1,053	2,433	95·1
Committed from prison by Lord Lieutenant's warrant:—				
Became insane while undergoing sentence of imprisonment,	40	38	78	3·1
Found as dangerous lunatics,	16	—	16	0·6
Became insane after committal and before trial,	9	3	12	0·5
Acquitted as insane,	1	1	2	0·1
Committed by Secretary of State for War,	16	...	16	0·6

It appears that 95·1 per cent. of the lunatics were committed direct to asylums by Justices as dangerous with intent to commit crime, and that only 4·3 per cent. were sent by Lord Lieutenant's warrant; 16, or 0·6 per cent., were committed by the Secretary of State for War.

Reformatory Schools.

With respect to institutions for the prevention of crime, namely, Reformatory and Industrial Schools, the following statement deals with juvenile criminals under Reformatory control in the year 1894, compared with 1893.

Reformatory Schools. Number in confinement.

Number of Juveniles on the Rolls of Reformatories at end of year	End of 1894. Boys.	End of 1894. Girls.	End of 1894. Total for year.	End of 1893. Total.	Increase in 1894.	Decrease in 1894.
In School,	528	76	604	619	—	15
On Licence,	15	...	15	37	—	22
Detained in School, sentence expired,	—	—	—	1	—	1
Absconded, sentence unexpired,	4	—	4	8	—	4
In Prison,	2	—	2	6	—	4
Total,	549	76	625	671	—	46

From this table it appears that there was a decrease of 46 in the number of children on the rolls of Reformatory Schools in Ireland at the end of 1894, as compared with the number at the close of the preceding year, which was 71 below that for 31st December, 1892. There were 15 less in the schools under sentence; and 22 less on licence. Two of those on the rolls were in prison at the close of the year, as compared with six at the close of the year 1893. Four of those on the rolls at the close of 1894 had absconded, with sentence unexpired, being four less than the number under this heading in 1893.

The total number on the rolls at the close of the year 1894 was 625 (549 boys and only 76 girls). The number committed during the year was 135—120 boys and 15 girls—showing a decrease of 8 as compared with the committals for the preceding year, which was 7 under the number for the year 1892. The number of boys committed last year was 120, or 10 more than in the year 1893, and the number of girls 15, or 18 under the number for 1893, and one over that for 1892.

Part I. Criminal Statistics.

Chapter III. Offenders, &c., in Custody.

Social Condition on Admission. Table 22.

The social condition of the children committed in 1894 to Reformatories in Ireland is shown in the following table:—

—	Boys.	Girls.	Proportion per cent. Boys.	Proportion per cent. Girls.
Total committed,	120	15	100	100
Illegitimate, deserted, or both parents destitute or criminal,	2	2	1·7	13·3
Both parents alive, not included in foregoing,	61	6	50·8	40·0
One parent dead,	36	4	30·0	26·7
Both orphans,	21	3	17·5	20·0

Only 2 of the 120 boys, and 2 of the 15 girls come under the head of the illegitimate, the deserted, and those having both parents destitute or criminal. Those having both parents living, and who are not included in the foregoing, formed 51 per cent. of the boys and 40 per cent. of the girls. The orphans (including those having one parent dead) were 47 per cent. of boys and 47 per cent. of girls.

Degree of Education. Table 23.

The degree of education (on admission) of children committed to Reformatory Schools is shown in the following summary:—

—	Boys.	Girls.	Proportion per cent. Boys.	Proportion per cent. Girls.
Total committed,	120	15	100	100
Neither read nor write,	52	7	43·3	46·7
Read, or read and write imperfectly,	64	7	53·3	46·7
Read and write well,	4	1	3·3	6·6
Superior Instruction,	–	–	–	–

Want of education.

The want of education is seen from this summary, which shows that only 4 of the 120 boys and 1 of the 15 girls admitted could read and write well.

Industrial Schools.

Industrial schools. Table 27.

Excluding Lunatic Asylums, the institutions in which the largest number of persons were in custody at the end of the year were Industrial Schools.

The total number of Industrial Schools in 1894 was 70, being equal to the number in 1893. Of the 70 schools 27 were in Munster, 19 in Leinster, 13 in Connaught, and 11 in Ulster.

Number in confinement.

The following summary shows the number of children under warrant of detention in Industrial Schools in Ireland at the end of 1894, as compared with similar statistics for the end of 1893:—

Children on the Rolls of Industrial Schools in Ireland.	End of 1894. Boys.	End of 1894. Girls.	End of 1894. Total.	End of 1893.	Increase, 1894.	Decrease, 1894.
In School,	[illegible]	[illegible]	[illegible]	[illegible]	–	[illegible]
On Licence,	327	336	663	[illegible]	–	[illegible]
Absconded,	3	...	3	[illegible]	–	[illegible]
Detained in school, sentence expired,	[illegible]	[illegible]	58	[illegible]	–	[illegible]
Total,	3,703	4,860	8,563	8,583	–	20

It appears from this table that the number of children on the rolls of Industrial Schools in Ireland at the end of 1894 (8,563) showed a slight decline from the number

(3,583) at the end of 1893. Of the total number, 3,318 were in the schools undergoing their sentence of detention, 68 were retained in school with their own consent although their sentences had expired, 669 were on licence, and 8 (all boys) had absconded.

Part I. Criminal Statistics. — Chapter III. Criminals, &c., in Confinement and at large. — Ages.

The following figures show the ages of the children placed in these schools in 1894 :—

Ages of Children.	Boys and Girls.	Boys.	Girls.	Percentage of Total.	
				Boys.	Girls.
Total,	1,277	604	673	100·	100·
Under 6 years,	44	10	34	1·7	5·0
6 and under 8 years,	343	143	200	23·7	29·7
8 and under 10 years,	385	181	206	30·0	29·7
10 and under 12 years,	323	177	146	29·3	21·4
12 years and upwards,	153	75	73	12·4	11·3

It appears from these figures that 67 per cent. of the girls and 39 per cent. of the boys were brought under careful training in these schools at the early age of under ten years.

In 1893, 639 girls were sent to Industrial Schools, as compared with 620 boys; and during last year, 673 girls were sent, as compared with 604 boys.

Table 8 exhibits statistics of the number of known thieves, depredators, receivers of stolen goods, and suspected persons at large and of the houses they frequent. There were in April last year 705 known thieves and depredators (495 males and 210 females), of whom 74 were under 16 years of age; 102 (55 males and 47 females) receivers of stolen goods; and 1,202 (810 males and 392 females) suspected persons, including 137 under 16 years of age.

Thieves, &c., at large. Table 8.

CHAPTER IV.—COST OF THE REPRESSION OF CRIME.

Chapter IV. Cost of Repressing Crime. Tables 1, 2, 20, 22, 24, 25, 26.

The cost of repression of crime is shown in the following statement :—

Cost of Repression of Crime.	1894.	1893.	Increase.	Decrease.
	£	£	£	£
Total cost,	2,697,748	2,683,263	14,485	–
Police,*	1,874,438	1,870,118	–	14,684
Prosecutions,†	96,244	93,233	3,011	–
Prisons,*	102,375	104,675	–	2,300
Criminal and Dangerous Lunatics,†	162,373	146,813	15,560	–
Industrial Schools,†	161,403	152,233	9,168	–
Reformatory Schools,†	25,897	25,843	–	54

* For year ended 31st March. † For year ended 31st December.

PART I. Judicial Statistics.

The following summary shows the Police Force in Ireland in 1894, compared with the number in 1893, at the periods of the year stated in the tables:—

Police Establishments. Table 1.

Constabulary and Police.	1893.	1894.	Increase, 1894.	Decrease, 1894.
Royal Irish Constabulary.				
Officers,	272	272	–	–
Head-Constables, Constables, &c.,	11,930	11,908	–	21
Total,	12,201	12,180	–	21
Dublin Metropolitan Police. (Table 2.)				
Superior Officers,	36	34	–	[illegible]
Sergeants, Constables, &c.,	1,198	1,198	–	–
Total,	1,234	1,232	–	[illegible]
Grand Total,	13,43[illegible]	13,402	–	23

Police Establishments. Tables 1 and 2.

A column in the first table in the Appendix shows the proportion which the number of effective force of Constabulary bears to the population (according to the Census of 1891) in the various counties, and in provincial towns with a separate Police force, in Ireland. In the following counties the proportion of Police to population is the smallest, as will be seen from the table:—

Dublin, . . . 12 in every 10,000 of the population in 1891.
Londonderry, . . . 13 " "
Down, . . . 13 " "
Armagh, . . . 13 " "
Tyrone, . . . 15 " "

Proportion of Police to population. Tables 1 and 2.

In the following counties in Ireland the proportion of Police is the largest:—

Clare, . . . 42 in every 10,000 of the population in 1891.
Westmeath, . . . 40 "
Limerick, . . . 40 "
Meath, . . . 37 "

The proportion of Police in the principal Cities and Towns is as follows:—

Galway, . . . 44 in every 10,000 of the population in 1891.
Waterford, . . . 34 "
Belfast City, Force, . . . 33 "
Dublin Metropolitan Police District, . . . 35 "
Drogheda, . . . 30 "
Kilkenny, . . . 28 "
Londonderry, . . . 27 "
Cork, . . . 24 "
Limerick, . . . 23 "

The proportion of Police—excluding County Inspectors and District Inspectors but including Depot and Reserve Force—to the estimated population of Ireland in 1894 was 28 in every 10,000 of the people.

In the Royal Irish Constabulary the members of the different branches of the Force are selected for special duty when necessary; in the Police of the Dublin Metropolitan Police District an entire division consisting of 32 officers with [illegible] detective officers, 19 Constables, and 10 Sergeants, 4 Inspectors, and 1 Superintendent, are employed as detectives.

Part I. Criminal Statistics. Criminal Cost of Repressing Crime. Detectives.

The following table shows the total cost of the Police Establishments in Ireland for the year ended 31st March, 1894, as compared with that for the preceding year:—

Cost of Establishments. Tables 1 and 2.

Cost of Police Establishments.	1893.	1894.	Increase, 1894.	Decrease, 1894.
	£	£	£	£
Total of all Ireland,	1,553,898	1,539,[illegible]	–	14,526
Royal Irish Constabulary,	1,403,180	1,390,078	–	13,102
Dublin Metropolitan Police,	148,[illegible]	149,[illegible]	–	1,424

This table indicates **a decrease of £14,526 in the total cost of the Police Force,** following a decrease of £10,862 **in the year ended 31st March, 1893.**

The demand for extra Constabulary during the year ended 30th September, 1894, was very much below the average for the preceding five years; the greatest number chargeable in any month was 1,[illegible] in November, 1893, as against 1,235 in August, 1893; 1,497 in October, 1891; 1,[illegible] in November, 1890; 1,784 in October, 1889; and 1,827 in October, 1888; the least number chargeable, 958 in September, 1894, was 144 under the minimum for the preceding year, and 68 under that for the year 1891-2.

Extra Constabulary. Table L. Part IV.

The cost of criminal lunatics and dangerous lunatics charged with an intention to commit a crime, is £157,810, or £14,249 **over** the amount for the preceding year, which amount was £1,238 under the cost for the year 1892.

Cost of Criminal Lunatics in Asylums. Table [illegible].

In the case of Industrial Schools, the total expenditure returned is £159,929—Imperial Taxes, £97,428;* Local Rates, £39,020;* other sources, £23,921, being an increase of £6,766 as compared with the amount for the year 1893, following a decrease of £11,870 in that year as compared with 1892.

Cost of Industrial Schools. Table 37.

The following table shows the cost of criminal classes, other than lunatics, in confinement in 1894, as compared with 1893:—

Cost of Criminals in Confinement. Tables 19 and 21.

Cost of Criminal Classes in Confinement.	1893.	1894.	Increase, 1894.	Decrease, 1894.
	£	£	£	£
Total of places of confinement,	117,973	111,619	–	6,314
Prisons,†	103,276	98,076	–	5,200
Reformatories,‡	14,697	15,043	–	64

* The sum (£137,013) entered under "Imperial Taxes" and "Local Rates" includes £733 unexpended at close of year.

† For year ended 31st March. ‡ For year ended 31st December.

PART I. CRIMINAL STATISTICS. CHAPTER IV. *Cost of Repressing Crime.* State Prisons. Table 93. Reformatories, Table 94. Costs of Criminal Prosecutions. Table 95.

The cost of State Prisons in Ireland (including Convict Prisons, Larger and Minor Local Prisons, and Bridewells), for the year ended 31st March, 1894, was £96,976, showing a decrease of £3,300, as compared with the cost for the preceding year, and £6,209 under the cost for the year ended 31st March, 1892.

As to Reformatories, the total costs in Ireland for the year 1894, are returned as £15,643—£9,681 charged to Imperial Taxes,* £4,831 to Local Rates,* and £1,361 to other sources—being £54 under the amount for the year 1893, which was £1,476 under that for 1892.

The form of return as to costs of criminal prosecutions, settled in 1872, has been continued. It brings the information up to 31st March, 1894.

Criminal Courts.	Costs of Criminal Prosecutions.		Increase, 1893-94.	Decrease, 1893-94.
	1892-93.	1893-94.		
	£	£	£	£
Total of all Ireland, ...	20,844	[illegible]	2,044	-
Assizes and Commission Courts, . .	[illegible]	19,169	3,549	-
Quarter Sessions, ...	8,348	[illegible]	-	419
Petty Sessions, Inquests, and Police Courts, ...	2,094	1,904	-	189

This table shows an increase in the cost of criminal prosecutions in Ireland in 1893-94 of £2,044, following a decrease of £6,638 in 1892-3, and an increase of £1,618 in 1891-92.

* The sum (£14,512), entered under "Imperial Taxes" and "Local Rates" includes £170 unexpended at the close of the year.

PART II.—JUDICIAL STATISTICS.

The Tables in this part include Statistics relating to the Civil Jurisdiction of all Courts in Ireland.

The Courts and Offices are divided into those which relate to the Central Administration of Justice, and those which relate to the Local Administration of Justice. The latter are classified into larger and smaller District Administration of Justice, according to the size of the districts into which Ireland is divided for the Special Jurisdiction.

I.—CENTRAL ADMINISTRATION OF JUSTICE.

The Central Administration of Justice includes the High Court of Justice, which consists of four divisions—Chancery, Queen's Bench, Exchequer, and the Probate and Matrimonial Division.

There are three outlying Courts:—The Court of the Land Commission, the High Court of Admiralty, and the Court of Bankruptcy.

The Central Appellate Jurisdictions, viz., Her Majesty's Court of Appeal, Ireland; Court for Crown Cases Reserved; Court for Cases Reserved for Judges of the Queen's Bench and Exchequer Divisions; the Privy Council in Ireland; Her Majesty in Council; and the House of Lords; have been grouped along with the other Central Jurisdictions, as they are closely connected with them.

The chief business of the Queen's Bench and Exchequer Divisions (the proceedings at the Plea side) is given in consecutive tables. The Statistics regarding the exclusive jurisdiction of each of the divisions:—at the Crown side of the Queen's Bench, as to election petitions and acknowledgments of married women in the same division, and at the Revenue side of the Exchequer, are given last, as the business is so small, compared with that transacted on the Plea side of these divisions.

The proceedings of Jury Trials in Dublin of these divisions; the Dublin County Court Appeals; the proceedings at chambers before a single Judge; and the applications to have cases of minor importance remitted to County Courts form another group.

The offices of Registration of Judgments and Local Registration of Title are grouped together, and along with them is given the Registry of Deeds, as the functions performed by all three are somewhat similar.

Part II. [illegible]

The statistics as to the Chancery, Common Law, and Land Judges' Taxing Offices are given in one Table, the offices having been consolidated.

As the business of the Receiver's Office of the Land Judges corresponds with a large part of the business of the Registrar in Lunacy (that relating to the Accounting of Committees of Estates of Lunatics), the statistics of the two offices have been placed together.

The information from the Inland Revenue Department, as to all the law taxes, is included in one return.

High Court of Justice—Chancery Division.

Chancery Division. — Business in Court before Lord Chancellor, Master of the Rolls, and Vice-Chancellor. Tables 30, 31.

The following summary shows the Court business in the Chancery Division during the years 1883 and 1884, with the increase or decrease under each head in the latter year.

Court Business in Chancery Division.	1883.	1884.	Increase, 1884.	Decrease, 1884.
Before Lord Chancellor.				
[N.B.—The Lord Chancellor sat constantly as President of the Court of Appeal during five days of the week. He also exercises under the Queen's Sign Manual the sole jurisdiction in Lunacy. For his Orders, made in that Department, see p. 54 infra.]				
Orders on motions specially from Chambers,	29	37	8	—
Orders on motions of course,	8	2	—	6
Orders on petitions of course,	—	—	—	—
Orders on petitions heard,	2	2	—	—
Causes, motions, &c., heard,	—	—	—	—
Motions for decree or judgment heard,	—	—	—	—
Causes, motions, &c., for further consideration heard,	—	—	—	—
	38	40	3	—
Before Master of the Rolls.				
Orders on motions specially from Chambers,	248	241	—	7
Orders on motions of course,	178	158	—	20
Orders on petitions heard,	28	28	—	—
Causes, motions, &c., heard,	41	39	—	2
Motions for decree or judgment heard,	32	30	—	2
Causes, motions, &c., for further consideration heard,	23	23	—	—
	[illegible]	[illegible]	—	[illegible]
Before Vice-Chancellor.				
Orders on motions specially from Chambers,	345	321	—	24
Orders on motions of course,	159	147	—	12
Orders on petitions heard,	23	33	10	—
Orders on County Court Appeals,	2	2	—	—
Causes, motions, &c., heard,	29	31	2	—
Motions for decree or judgment heard,	38	25	—	13
Causes, motions, &c., for further consideration heard,	15	16	1	—
County Court equity appeals heard,*	—	2	2	—
	611	585	—	26
Total,	1,[illegible]	1,959	—	73

This table shows a decrease of Court business of 73 proceedings, following a decrease of 28 in 1883.

Registrars' Office. Table 32.

In the office of the Registrars of the Chancery Division, the total number of Side Bar Orders was 193, or 8 over the number for 1883.

* There were also 3 of such Appeals before the Lord Judge in 1884.

From the County Court equitable jurisdiction, up to £500 property and £30 a year in land, there were 5 Appeals filed, which, with 1 pending at the end of 1893, gave 6 as the number of such Appeals for hearing during the year, and of those, 3 were dismissed with costs or affirmed, 1 was remitted, 1 was struck out, and the remaining 1 was pending at the end of the year. Part II. Judicial Statistics. Central Administration of Justice.

The following is a summary of the principal proceedings in the chambers of the Lord Chancellor, the Master of the Rolls, and the Vice-Chancellor:— Chancery Division. Chief Clerk's Records of proceedings in Chambers. Table 32.

Proceedings in Chambers of Chancery Judges.	1893.	1894.	Increase, 1894.	Decrease, 1894.
Summonses:—				
To make Infants Wards,	21	22	—	1
For the Administration of Estates,	193	173	20	—
Under the Charitable Trusts Act,	—	—	—	—
For appointment of Guardians and maintenance of Infants / For other purposes,	135	108	27	—
Other Summonses than to originate Proceedings,	1,600	1,788	—	188
Appointments (by Summonses, &c.), disposed of,	3,323	3,410	—	87
Orders made:—				
Of the Class drawn up by the Registrars,	—	—	—	—
Of the Class drawn up in Chambers,	1,443	1,383	60	—
Orders brought into Chambers for prosecution:—				
Other than Orders for winding up Companies,	315	394	—	81
For winding up Companies,	3	4	—	1
Number of Advertisements issued,	206	132	—	74
Receivers' and Trustees' Accounts passed,	30	44	—	14
Receipts therein,	£136,850	£150,003	—	£13,153
Disbursements and allowances therein,	£108,312	£102,879	—	£[illegible]
Accounts passed other than Receivers' Accounts:—				
Number of Accounts,	222	276	—	54
Receipts therein,	£4,189,297	£877,118	—	£3,312,179
Disbursements and allowances therein,	£4,284,780	£861,896	—	£3,422,884

The amount of property passed in accounts fell from £4,416,335, in 1893, to £898,304, being a decrease of £3,518,031, following an increase of £3,305,087 in 1893, as compared with 1892.

In the Lord Chancellor's, the Master of the Rolls', and the Vice-Chancellor's Chambers there were at the end of the year 733 Wards of Court. The new Minor Matters in the year were 15, relating to 42 Minors as compared with 27 new Matters and 53 new Wards in 1893. Minor matters in Chambers.

The number of actions by writ of summons was 496, showing an increase of 20 over the number (476) in 1893. The proportion of lower scale to higher scale was as 82 to 18 per cent. The originating summonses (271) are 37 more than the summonses filed (234) in 1893. In the Notice Department there were 11,362 original documents, being 1,481 under the number of 12,843, and 42,409 copies, against 42,941 in 1893. Writs of Summons and Writs. Table 33.

The Lord Chancellor made 44 orders on Petitions as to Commissioners for administering oaths for the High Court of Justice. There were 7 orders on Petitions as to Notaries. The orders as to other Petitions, including Minor Matters, were 98. The warrants for Magistrates were 334, as compared with 393 in 1893, and 331 in 1892; the warrants as to Coroners were 7.

The return of the Secretary at the Rolls gives the particulars of 67 petitions set down for hearing before the Master of the Rolls. It appears that 21 of these were under the Trustee Acts, and 7 under the Public Works and Railway Acts.

In the Crown and Hanaper Office there were 3,527 official acts during the year 1894, as compared with 3,580 in 1893.

. . . .

. . .

LAND JUDGE.

Under the Land Judge the net rental or annual value (where given) of Estates sold in the year ended 1st November, 1894, was £23,052, as compared with £23,610 in 1893, £38,980 in 1892, £28,699 in 1891, £19,895 in 1890, £21,269 in 1889, £16,559 in 1888, and £17,974 in 1887, and the purchase money was £442,980, as compared with £393,185 in 1893, £506,880 in 1892, £410,401 in 1891, £342,418 in 1890, £402,023 in 1889, £278,442 in 1888, and £270,522 in 1887. As the properties sold did not consist solely of fee simple lands, the several amounts here set forth include the purchase money of life estates and other limited terms as well as of lands in fee.

The number of cases pending at the end of the year in the Judge's Chamber was 2,283 as compared with 2,313 in 1893.

There were 138 petitions filed in the year ended 31st October, 1894, being 34 under the number in the preceding year, only 27 being by owners. The number of affidavits filed was 3,090, against 3,965 in 1893.

The number of abstracts of title lodged was 121, and the number of deeds and other documents lodged 4,427.

QUEEN'S BENCH AND EXCHEQUER DIVISIONS.

The proceedings at the Plea side of the Queen's Bench and Exchequer Divisions are arranged in a single table for each division, although the figures have been supplied by three officers—the Clerk of Writs, the Master, and the Registrar.

The total number of writs of summons for the two divisions showed a decrease of 1,606 from 19,123 in 1893 to 17,517, following an increase of 1,074 in 1893 as compared with 1892. The number of cases which actually came to trial by jury in Dublin in 1894 was 244, being 10 under the number in 1893; the amount of money recovered at these trials shows a decrease from £22,454 in 1893 to £18,130, following an increase of £8,684 in 1893, as compared with 1892.

Of the other business of the Divisions on the Plea side, there were 17,014 affidavits, being 954 under the number for 1893, which was an increase of 614 on that for 1892.

At Chambers there were 228 summonses against 208 in 1893, and 216 in 1892. The motions on notice before a single Judge numbered 323 or 21 less than in the preceding year. The number of ex parte motions, including consent orders, granted before a single Judge, was 1,385, being a decrease of 170 as compared with the number in 1893, which was 58 over the number in 1892.

The Judges for Jury trials in Dublin also hear Appeals from the Courts of the Recorder, the County Court Judge for the City and County of Dublin.

The statistics of these appeals or rehearings in 1893 and 1894 are as follows:—

Appeals (Rehearings).		Entered.	Affirmed.	Dismissed.	Settled, Struck out, &c.	Reversed.
From Decree or Dismiss of Recorder of Dublin City and County Dublin (including cases stated),	1893,	63	46	24	17	–
	1894,	85	51	13	21	1

The proceedings as to applications to have **cases remitted to County Courts are as** follows:—

Proceedings under Sect. [illegible]	1893.	1894.	Increase, 1894.	Decrease, 1894.
Number of applications to remit to Inferior Courts,	415	386	–	29
Number of applications refused,	63	61	–	2
Number of applications granted,	352	325	–	[illegible]
In Cases of Contract under £50.				
Number of applications granted,	135	120	–	**15**
In Cases of Tort.				
Number of applications granted under sec. 6,	[illegible]	205	–	[illegible]

It appears from this table that the number of applications to remit cases to the County Courts was 386, showing a decrease of 29 as compared with the year 1893, the number for which year was 56 in excess of that for 1892. Of the 325 applications granted, 120 were in cases of contract and 205 in cases of tort.

The business of the Judges of the High Court on Circuit is dealt with at page 49.

Queen's Bench Division.

The Queen's Coroner, Attorney and Master on the Crown side has made his usual return of the business at the Crown side of the Queen's Bench. See Table 47.

There were no election petitions in 1894.

No acknowledgments by married women have been filed during either of the last two years; in the year 1892 three were filed. Under the provisions of the Conveyancing Act, 1882 (45 & 46 Vic., cap. 39, sec. 7), no Certificates and Affidavits of Acknowledgments are filed, save such as relate to Deeds executed before the commencement of the Act.

Two Perpetual Commissioners were appointed during 1894; in the preceding year no such appointments were made. There were 10 Special Commissions granted in 1894, being equal to the number in 1893.

Part II. Judicial Statistics. — General Administration of Justice. — Exchequer Division. — Revenue Side. Tables 41 and 42.

Exchequer Division.

The writs issued on the Revenue side were 421, as compared with 469 in 1893. The Side Bar Rules were 46, as compared with 31 in 1893, 57 in 1892, and 54 in 1891. The affidavits filed were 136, being 9 over the number in 1893.

Registry of Judgments Office. Table 51.

Offices of Registration.

The number of judgments, &c., registered in the Registry of Judgments Office in 1894, as compared with the preceding year, was as follows:—

Registry of Judgments Office.	1893.	1894.	Increase, 1894.	Decrease, 1894.
Judgments of Superior Courts registered,	2,7[illegible]	2,451	–	281
" " re-registered,	71	184	113	–
Revivals,	[illegible]	–	–	[illegible]
Decrees, Rules, and Orders,	–	–	–	–
Lispendens registered,	2,1[illegible]	2,407	2[illegible]7	–
" re-registered,	57	73	16	–
Judgments from Courts in England and Scotland registered,	5	[illegible]	–	[illegible]
Do. judicial, Irish Land Commission,	18	–	–	18
Total,	4,986	5,102	116	–
Recognizances registered,	198	155	–	43
" re-registered,	96	43	–	53
Crown Bonds registered,	99	65	–	[illegible]
" re-registered,	67	–	–	67
Total,	460	263	–	19[illegible]
Satisfactions of Judgments,	89	82	–	7
Vacates of Recognizances, and Cancellations of Crown Bonds,	150	105	–	45
Negative Searches, 5s. Stamps,	1	2	1	–
" " 10s. Stamps,	2,180	[illegible]	860	–
" " 2s. 6d. Stamps,	55	[illegible]	–	34
Total,	[illegible]	[illegible]	[illegible]	–
Requisitions for Liberty to search made by public,	[illegible]	[illegible]	–	[illegible]
Stamped Certificates issued,	[illegible]	[illegible]	–	141

The figures in the above table show an increase of business in some departments of the office, and a decrease in others. The number of Judgments of the Irish Superior Courts registered was 2,451, being 281 under the number for the year 1893, which was 142 in excess of that for 1892.

In the latter part of 1893 the compulsory registration of Recognizances, as a charge against Real Estate was dispensed with, unless specially ordered.

None of the Judgments registered in 1894 were obtained before 15th July, 1850 (which judgments alone affect land without being registered in the Deeds Office as a Judgment Mortgage); of the 184 Judgments re-registered, 182 were obtained before 15th July, 1850, and only 2 since that date.

PART II. JUDICIAL STATISTICS. — General Administration of Justice.

On comparing the number of judgments registered with the number of executions issued on Judgments in the Queen's Bench and Exchequer Divisions, it appears that 5,636 judgment executions are returned in the proceedings in Masters' Offices as entered up, and that 2,451 judgments were registered in the Registry of Judgments Office.

Local Registration of Title Office. Table 32.

Table 32 contains a return of proceedings in the Local Registration of Title (Ireland) Office, under 54 and 55 Vic., cap. 66, for the year **1894**. During the year there were [illegible]—[illegible] compulsory, and 17 voluntary—applications **to** register in cases completed by the Land Commission before the end of 1891 (in **which a** written application and examination of the Title are required). The total number **of** current cases (i.e., **cases** sent down from day to day by the Land Commission, **and** registered **as of** course, no application being necessary), and application cases registered during the year was 3,8[illegible]. In the year also 2,369 Titles were read, and 3,820 Searches issued. In the two years, 1892 and 1893, which were the first years during which the **Act of 1891** was **in** operation, 8,627 cases were registered, 5,420 Titles read, and 4,041 Searches issued.

Bills of Sale. Table 32.

Bills of Sale are registered by the Master of the Queen's Bench Division, and included in the return of business at the Plea side. They are grouped here with the business in other offices of registration. The number of bills of sale was 311, as compared with 327 in 1893, and 340 in 1892.

Registry of Deeds Table 33.

The number of deeds registered in the Registry of Deeds Office **in the year was 23,904**, as compared with 24,315 in 1893, and 24,412 in 1892. Judgment Mortgage Affidavits are included in this number; they amounted to 438, as compared with 485 in 1893. The searches made by the public were 5,001; those lodged for official search were 3,887, of which 1,481 were negative searches, and 2,406 common searches. The abstract book, entered up to 14th December in 1893, was, on the 31st of December, 1894, entered up to 18th December. In 1893 the Lands Index was entered to 2nd of December, and in 1894 it was entered to 23rd November. The Transcription of Memorials was completed to 11th of December in 1893, and to 23rd November in 1894. The negative searches lodged but not made were 10 in 1893, and 18 in 1894, and the common searches lodged but not made numbered 28 in the former and 32 in the latter **year.**

The negative searches made and ready for delivery but not taken out amounted to 423, and the common searches to 82.

TAXATION OF COSTS.

Taxation of Costs. Table 34.

The Costs taxed in the Consolidated Taxing Offices, **and certified, amounted** to £238,152. The corresponding amount for 1893 was **£242,329, which shows a** decrease of £4,187 for last year, following a decrease of £13,886 **in 1893, as compared with** 1892.

APPOINTMENT OF RECEIVERS.

Receivers under Land Judge. Table 35.

There were 63 new receivers appointed by the Land Judge (or other Judge of the High Court, but accounting to the Land Judge), as compared with 96 in 1893, 74 in 1892, 90 in 1891, 148 in 1890, 156 in 1889, 154 in 1888, 192 in 1887, 129 in 1886, 310 in 1885, 177 in 1884, 181 in 1883, and 165 in 1882. The total number under the Land Judge at the end of the year was 1,268 as compared with 1,405 at the end of 1893, and 1,450 at the end of 1892.

The year's rental under the Court of the receivers and guardians who passed accounts, which are filed in the Consolidated Record and Writ Office, is £291,645, of which £151,866 was in lunacy matters, and £139,780 in other actions and suits.

It appears that there were 884 lettings by proposal without biddings; there was not a single letting by biddings. Of the 884 lettings, 243 were for 7 years, pending the cause, and 641 were for shorter periods.

PART II. Judicial Statistics. Central Administration of Justice. Lunacy Department. Table 58.

The chief business in the Lunacy Department in 1894 compared with 1893 was as follows:—

Lunacy Office.	1893.	1894.	Increase, 1894.	Decrease, 1894.
Orders of the Lord Chancellor, including Fiats confirming Registrar's Reports,	556	509	–	47
Affidavits filed,*	[illegible]	[illegible]	–	–
Reports of Registrar,	110	114	–	–
Accounts, &c., passed by Registrar,	159	214	55	–
	£	£	£	£
Gross income of Lunatics,	[illegible]	[illegible]	[illegible]	–

* Not including affidavits verifying Petitions and Accounts.

The number of Orders (509) was 47 under that for the year 1893, and 57 under **the number for 1892.**

The number of lunatics under the control of the Lord Chancellor at the close of 1894 **was 366, being 7 over the number at the close of 1893.**

PROBATE AND MATRIMONIAL DIVISION.

Principal Registry. Table 57.

The following is a summary of the business of the Court of Probate in Ireland and the Principal Registry:—

COURT OF PROBATE—PRINCIPAL REGISTRY.	1893.	1894.	Increase, 1894.	Decrease, 1894.
Probates and administrations with Will annexed,	1,471	1,651	180	–
Administrations without Will,	999	1,085	86	–
Total probates and administrations,	2,470	2,736	266	–
Caveats,	649	661	12	–
Actions instituted,	59	71	12	–
Trials by special jury,	9	14	5	–
Trials by common jury,	16	14	–	2
Causes heard without a jury,	22	22	–	–
Court Motions,	304	228	–	76
Petitions,	51	55	4	–
	£	£	£	£
Total amount of fees received,	8,450	[illegible]	577	–

From the above it appears that there was an increase of 266 in probates and letters of administration in 1894 as compared with 1893; the number **for** which year was 316 under that for 1892.

The taxation of costs is now included in the returns of the Consolidated Taxing Office.

Comptroller of Stamps' Return as to Property under Probate, &c. Table 59.

A return received from the Comptroller of Stamp Duties shows the amount of duty paid for Grants of Probate and Administration in 1894 to be £205,649, namely, £138,858 in Dublin, and £67,791 in the country districts, as compared with £182,655, namely, £118,291 in Dublin, and £64,364 in the country districts, in 1893, being an increase of £22,994, following a decrease of £66,831 in 1893 as compared with 1892.

As to matrimonial causes and matters and proceedings under the Legitimacy Declaration Act (Ireland), 1868, it appears that there were 29 petitions filed in matrimonial causes and matters during the year; 11 citations were issued. The only decrees were 2 for divorce a mensa et thoro, and 1 for restitution of conjugal rights. There were 31 motions and 3 causes heard in the year. There was no petition under the Legitimacy Declaration Act. Part II. Judicial Statistics. Central Administration of Justice. Jurisdiction in Matrimonial causes. Table 58.

High Court of Admiralty.

The causes instituted in the High Court of Admiralty in Ireland in the year were 15, as compared with 14 in 1893, and 12 in 1892. There were 8 causes pending at end of 1893, making 23 in all to be disposed of. Admiralty. Tables 59 and 60.

The motions and summonses heard were 72, final judgments and decrees 9, and instruments, &c., prepared in the Registry 53; showing a total of 141, being 55 over the total in 1893, and 65 over that for 1892.

Court of Bankruptcy.

In the following summary the principal proceedings in Bankruptcy in the Court of Bankruptcy, Dublin, and the Local Courts in Belfast and Cork constituted under the Local Bankruptcy (Ireland) Act, 1888, are compared with those of the preceding year. Bankruptcy. Tables 61 and 62.

Proceedings in Bankruptcy.	Court of Bankruptcy, Dublin.		Local Court, Belfast.		Local Court, Cork.		The three Courts.			
							Total.		Increase, 1894.	Decrease, 1894.
	1893.	1894.	1893.	1894.	1893.	1894.	1893.	1894.		
Petitions of Bankruptcy:										
By Creditors,	102	93	19	20	10	10	131	116	—	15
By Debtors,	24	22	4	7	4	2	32	31	—	1
Private arrangements turned into Bankruptcies,	33	38	8	9	1	5	42	52	10	—
Petitions for Arrangement,	213	203	31	32	18	12	264	247	—	17
Sittings before the Court,	5,807	5,282	608	438	19	14	6,434	5,740	—	[illegible]
Sittings before the Chief Registrar and the Chief Clerk in Dublin, and those before the Registrars in Belfast and in Cork,	2,784	2,820	446	436	187	258	3,418	3,488	—	[illegible]

Note.—The data in the Return for 1893, as regards "Sittings" before the Local Courts, have been amended.

It appears that the number of petitions of Bankruptcy in 1894 was 137, showing a decrease of 6 as compared with the number, 143, in 1893, which was 18 under that for 1892. The petitions for arrangement (including 52 private arrangements turned into Bankruptcy) was 247, being 17 under the number for 1893, which was 18 over that for 1892.

Details regarding the Bankruptcies and Insolvencies under the charge of each Official Assignee not finally wound up on the 31st December, 1894, are given in Tables 62 and 63.

Part II. Judicial Statistics.

General Administration of Justice.

FINANCE.

The Accountant-General, High Court of Justice, Chancery Division, carried over (in cash, securities, and other effects) on 1st of October, 1886, £3,176,599,* being £216,961 under the amount carried over on the corresponding day in 1885.

Accountant-General's Office, Table 66.

Table 67 contains particulars regarding the Receipts and Payments of the Accountant-General of the Supreme Court of Judicature in Ireland, in respect of the funds of suitors in said Court, and a statement of Liabilities and Assets in respect of such funds, also particulars of securities in Court.

Law Taxes. Table 68.

A Return has been obtained from the Inland Revenue Department of the Law Taxes levied in connexion with the High Court of Justice; see Table 68.

APPELLATE JURISDICTION.

Her Majesty's Court of Appeal, Ireland. Table 69.

The Proceedings in the Supreme Courts of Appeal, in 1886, are shown in Tables 69–74.

During the year 35 appeals from final judgments from Divisions of the High Court of Justice were heard and judgment delivered by Her Majesty's Court of Appeal in Ireland, 25 of which Appeals were from the Chancery, 5 from the Queen's Bench, 4 from the Exchequer, and one from the Probate and Matrimonial Causes Division. There were 42 appeals (including ex parte appeals) from interlocutory orders from Divisions of the High Court of Justice heard, viz. :—16 from the Chancery, 14 from the Queen's Bench, 10 from the Exchequer, and 2 from the Probate and Matrimonial Causes Division. Fifty-six appeals from other Judges or Courts were heard, 4 of which were from the Judges in Bankruptcy, 1 was from the High Court of Admiralty, 23 were Registry of Voters Appeals, 1 was a case stated pursuant to County Court Appeals (Ireland) Act, 1889, and 26 were appeals from the Irish Land Commission. There were also 61 original motions heard. The Judgments delivered were 133. In 21 of these the Judgment below was affirmed; in 33 it was reversed; in 1 reversed with declaration, direction, or finding; and in 3 cases varied.

Privy Council, Ireland. Table 72.

There were 13 applications to the Privy Council in Ireland for confirmation of provisional Orders made in pursuance of the "Labourers (Ireland) Acts, 1883 to 1892," and there were 4 such cases remaining from 1885; in 4 cases the Orders were confirmed, in 17 the orders were disallowed or varied, and 2 cases were pending at the close of the year. There were also before the Council 11 applications under the "Tramways and Light Railways (Ireland) Acts, 1860 to 1896;" 20 objections to Schemes framed in pursuance of the "Educational Endowments (Ireland) Act, 1885" (4 of which were confirmed, 2 were withdrawn, 3 were remitted to the Commissioners, and 11 cases were pending at the close of the year); 4 Petitions under the Fisheries (Ireland) Acts; one application under the Lunacy (Ireland) Acts; one application under the Grand Juries (Ireland) Act, 6 & 7 Wm. IV. c. 116; and one petition under the Loan Fund (Ireland) Act, 6 & 7 Vict. cap. 91.

Her Majesty in Council. Table 73.

There were no appeals from Ireland to Her Majesty in Council.

House of Lords. Table 74.

One application from Ireland was presented to the House of Lords in the year 1886, one cause was withdrawn, and one dismissed for want of prosecution.

Tables 20 and 71.

There were 2 appeals before the Judges of the Common Law Divisions, as to Precontracts and other cases not within the 11 & 12 Vic., cap. 78; the decision in one case was that the Precontract ought to be fixed, and in the other that it ought not; and there were also 2 cases before the Court for Crown Cases Reserved, in both of which the conviction was affirmed.

II.—LOCAL ADMINISTRATION OF JUSTICE—LARGER DISTRICTS.

Part II. Judicial Statistics. — Local Administration of Justice—Larger Districts.

Local Courts of Admiralty, Table 75. District Probate Registries, Table 76.

Admiralty jurisdiction.—In Belfast in 1894 there were only 4 actions or proceedings, being 4 under the number for the preceding year; and in Cork, 1 only, against 10 for the year 1893.

In the District Registries of the Court of Probate the chief business in 1893 and 1894 was as follows:—

Grants in Probate—District Registries.	1893.	1894.	Increase 1894.	Decrease 1894.
Granted in Common Form:				
Probates,	2,[illegible]	2,475	58	—
Letters of administration with the Will annexed,	319	316	5	—
Letters of administration—under Intestate Widows' Acts,	3	5	—	—
——— others,	2,033	2,148	110	—
Granted under direction of Judge:				
Probates,	9	16	1	
Letters of administration with the Will annexed,	12	6	—	5
Letters of administration,	22	13	—	8
Granted on Reports of County Court Judges:				
Probates,	16	20	1	—
Letters of administration with Will annexed,	2	4	—	1
Letters of administration,	6	4	—	1
Total granted,	5,[illegible]	5,497	181	—
Revoked or refused:				
Probates,	0	3	—	1
Letters of administration,	5	3	—	
	4	4	2	4
Total amount of fees received,	10,[illegible]	12,[illegible]	678	—
Amount of duty on Affidavits lodged for grants,	[illegible]	[illegible]	[illegible]	—

Number of probates of wills and letters of administration in Ireland.

There has been an increase of 181 in the number of wills proved and letters of administration granted in 1894, at the District Registries, of which there are eleven. This increase follows a decrease of 254 in 1893, as compared with 1892, and an increase of [illegible] in 1892 as compared with 1891. The aggregate number at both Central and District Registries (7,[illegible]) is 427 over the number for 1893, 287 under that for 1892, and [illegible] over the number for 1891.

Proving of Wills where estate small, at Offices of Inland Revenue.

The 33rd section of "The Customs and Inland Revenue Act, 1881," affords local facilities for obtaining grants of probate or letters of administration, where the gross value of the personal estate of the deceased does not exceed £500, and by section 16 of "The Finance Act, 1894," the limit has been extended to £[illegible]. In 1894 there were in Ireland 99 towns where officers of Inland Revenue were authorized to deal with applications under the provisions referred to.

For Proceedings in Local Bankruptcy Courts, Belfast and Cork, see page 17.

Proceedings on Circuit.

Proceedings on Circuit.

There are five circuits in Ireland, and Assizes are held in thirty-three towns. Six of these towns are counties of cities and towns with distinct Grand and Petit Juries and Officers. The Grand and Petit Juries of the county of the town of Carrickfergus are brought to Belfast for assize purposes, but those of Drogheda are not brought to Dundalk, the county town of Louth. The following statement contains a Summary of the Proceedings on Circuit during the year 1894.

PART II. JUDICIAL STATISTICS. — Local Administration of Justice — Equity Districts — Proceedings on Circuit, Tables 73, 77–81.

PROCEEDINGS ON CIRCUIT, 1894.

CIRCUITS, &c., AND COUNTIES [illegible]	Number of Appeals [illegible]	Proceedings [illegible]	[illegible] Appeals [illegible]	[illegible]
LEINSTER CIRCUIT:				
Carlow,	38	...	...	9
Kildare,	36	3	...	20
Kilkenny (County and City),	63	1	...	36
Queen's County,	34	...	1	11
Tipperary,	45	4	2	47
Waterford (County and City),	89	2	...	22
Wexford,	34	5	8	8
Wicklow,	20	5	...	11
Total,	3[illegible]3	17	8	1[illegible]5
MUNSTER CIRCUIT:				
Clare,	198	...	13	40
Cork (County and City),	231	30	11	81
Kerry,	288	2	7	45
Limerick (County and City),	118	6	7	36
Total,	[illegible]	38	38	169
NORTH-EAST CIRCUIT:				
Antrim (excluding Belfast and Carrickfergus),	196	30	23	137
Armagh,	128	6	...	26
Down,	107	1	3	35
Louth (and Drogheda),	32	3	...	16
Meath,	14	...	4	15
Monaghan,	100	2	3	6
Total,	5[illegible]	42	34	236
NORTH-WEST CIRCUIT:				
Cavan,	108	...	2	17
Donegal,	139	6	11	25
Fermanagh,	45	1	4	18
Londonderry (County and City),	124	24	2	41
Longford,	15	...	...	11
Tyrone,	250	4	18	23
Westmeath,	23	...	...	12
Total,	5[illegible]	36	38	130
CONNAUGHT CIRCUIT:				
Galway (County and Town),	223	4	10	55
King's County,	38	...	...	18
Leitrim,	114	1	1	20
Mayo,	250	1	2	24
Roscommon,	10[illegible]	4	...	17
Sligo,	116	5	...	14
Total,	[illegible]	19	15	1[illegible]
TOTAL OF IRELAND,	3,[illegible]	1[illegible]	160	[illegible]

* [illegible]

Jury Trials. Tables 77, 78, and 79. The number of causes entered for trial on circuit in 1894 was 154, being a decline of 61 as compared with that for the preceding year, and 14 under the number for the year 1892. The amount recovered, which had risen from £5,[illegible] in 1892 to £18,[illegible] in 1893, fell to £5,[illegible] last year.

Appeals from County Court Judges. Table 81. The Appeals from County Court Judges and Recorders numbered 3,43[illegible] in 1893, and 3,[illegible] in 1894.

173

There were in 1894, 12 objections to Presentments heard by Judges, and 16 special directions given.

Railway traverses under the Railway Acts, which had risen from 31 in 1892 to 45 in 1893, fell again last year to 31, and of these, 13 were in the County of Clare. There were three tramway traverses under Tramway Acts in 1893, and none in 1894. The traverses other than railway and tramway traverses, which in 1893 were 104 in number, fell last year to 35—£5,640 was claimed in the cases where verdicts were given, and £2,365 found by verdict.

The memorials from persons fined for non-attendance as Jurors fell from 62 in 1893 to 52 in 1894. The fines appealed from in cases heard were £127 in 1893, and £114 in 1894. In both years the fines in cases heard were altogether remitted.

Part II. Judicial Statistics. Fiscal administration of Justice. Railway, Tramway, and other traverses on circuit. Table 49. Fines on Jurors on circuit. Table 50. Process servers. Table 52.

County Courts.

Returns have been obtained from all the Process Servers (804) appointed under statute by the County Court Judges and Recorders, and whose salary is annually voted by Parliament.

The Civil Bill ejectments served by these officers are 12,714 as compared with 14,018 in 1893, 17,546 in 1892, 16,067 in 1891, 17,090 in 1890, 18,083 in 1889, 25,481 in 1888, 26,836 in 1887, 31,064 in 1886, 18,539 in 1885, and 23,558 in 1884; the number of replevins, 184, as compared with 438 in 1893, 316 in 1892, 285 in 1891, 280 in 1890, 198 in 1889, 180 in 1888, 348 in 1887, 294 in 1886, 430 in 1885, and 312 in 1884; and the number of other civil bills, 184,615, as compared with 192,427 in 1893, 188,974 in 1892, 172,990 in 1891, 156,704 in 1890, 187,730 in 1889, 199,689 in 1888, 211,408 in 1887, 211,825 in 1886, 228,193 in 1885, and 226,494 in 1884.

The statistics of proceedings (other than at Equity or Land Sessions, or under Local Admiralty Jurisdiction Act, or the Local Bankruptcy (Ireland) Act, 1888), in the Courts of County Court Judges and Courts of Recorders whether ejectments, causes remitted from the Superior Courts, or other suits, have been collected into one Table.

County Court Proceedings. Table 53.

In ejectments entered there was a decrease of 1,584 in 1894, following an increase of 1,193 in 1893.

Ejectments.

	Ejectments Entered.
For 1893,	15,258
For 1894,	13,674
Decrease in 1894,	1,584

In cases remitted from the Superior Courts which were entered below there was a decrease from 344 in 1893 to 286 in 1894. In other suits there was a decrease of 3,750 from 93,766 in 1893 to 89,016 in 1894, following an increase of 3,116 between 1892 and 1893, and an increase of 2,756 between 1891 and 1892. There were only 58 cases disposed of by a jury.

Cases Remitted.

The amount decreed in the Civil Bill Courts in 1894 was £214,680 in ejectment cases, and £400,956 in other suits, making £620,636.[1] Compared with 1893, the amount decreed in ejectment cases shows a decrease of £56,366, and the amount decreed in other suits a decrease of £26,189. The costs adjudged to plaintiffs amounted to £52,964, being £4,136 under the amount in 1893. Of these costs, £17,057 was in ejectment cases, and £35,907 in other suits.

Ordinary Civil Bills.

The Equitable Jurisdiction cases for 1894 (exclusive of Lunacy Proceedings), were 776 as compared with 809 cases for 1893.

In County Court Lunacy Cases, under the jurisdiction conferred by the Lunacy Act of 1880, there were 67 orders made.

Local equitable petitions [illegible]. Table 54. County Court Lunacy Jurisdiction.

[1] Including £[illegible] at Land Sessions, under the Landlord and Tenant (Ireland) Act, 1870, the total was £[illegible].

Part II. Judicial Statistics. — Local Administration of Justice. — County Courts, &c.

A classification of the ejectments executed by Sheriffs and Special Bailiffs according as they came from the High Court of Justice or the County Courts, gives the following results:—

Ejectments executed by Sheriffs, &c. Table 85.

	High Courts				County Courts			
	1893.	1894.	Increase.	Decrease.	1893.	1894.	Increase.	Decrease.
Ejectments executed,	439	422	–	17	2,324	2,170	–	154
Leinster,	169	213	44	–	598	476	–	122
Munster,	284	157	–	127	742	699	–	43
Ulster,	86	21	–	65	530	517	–	13
Connaught,	36	31	–	5	454	478	24	–

The ejectments executed show a decrease of 171—from 2,763 in 1893 to 2,592 last year, following an increase of 150 in 1893 as compared with 1892.

In the ejectments from the High Court which were executed the total number (422) shows a decrease of 17 as compared with the ejectments for 1893, the number for which year was 52 over that for 1892.

County Court Ejectment Suits and Executions compared.

The County Court Ejectment Suits entered and lodged, which had risen from 12,418 in 1892, to 13,626 in 1893, fell last year to 12,074, the last number thus showing a decrease of 1,552 as compared with that for 1893.

The executions of County Court ejectments show a decrease of 154—from 2,324 in 1893 to 2,170 last year. The number for 1893 was 190 over that for 1892.

Eviction Notices. Table 86.

The total number of Eviction Notices filed during the year 1894, under Section 7 of the Land Law (Ireland) Act, 1887, was 5,473, being 1,095 under the number for 1893, which was 1,128 over that for 1892. Of the 5,473 notices last year, 110 were filed in the High Court of Justice, and 5,363 in County Courts.

The number of Civil Bill decrees and dismisses returned as executed during last year is 20,998, of which 15,403 were executed by Sheriffs, and 5,595 by Special Bailiffs. In 1893 the number was 24,869, and in 1892 it was 20,548.

Warrants against Squatter Tenants and Weekly Tenants. Table 88.

The warrants to Special Bailiffs under Act 23 & 24 Vic., c. 154 (summary recovery of possession of tenements), were 1,155 in 1893 and 1,087 in 1894. The warrants to Special Bailiffs under 14 & 15 Vic., cap. 92, s. 15 (summary recovery of possession of tenements overheld in towns), 13,968, show a decrease of 173 from the number in 1893, which was 691 under that for the year 1892.

Summary recovery of possession of tenements overheld in towns. Ejectments executed for non-payment of rent and others in 1894 and 1893, compared. Table 87.

The following is a Summary of the Returns of Sheriffs as to execution of ejectments, classed so as to show the proportion that were and were not for non-payment of rent:—

	Ejectments for Non-payment of Rent.				Ejectments for other causes.			
	1893.	1894.	Increase 1894.	Decrease 1894.	1893.	1894.	Increase 1894.	Decrease 1894.
Ireland,	2,079	1,918	–	161	658	650	...	8
Leinster,	604	538	...	66	161	146	–	15
Munster,	739	638	–	101	237	172	–	65
Ulster,	342	364	22	...	183	214	31	–
Connaught,	411	397	...	14	77	118	41	–

From this Table it appears that there was a decrease of 161 in ejectments for non-payment of rent (following an increase of 218 in 1893), and a decrease of 8 in other ejectments.

The statistics as to the number of proceedings under the Landlord and Tenant Act of 1870, are shown in the following table:— Part II. Judicial Statistics.

Cases entered in Land Sessions.	1893.	1894.	Increase in 1894.	Decrease in 1894.
Total number of cases,	83	63	—	20
Decrees,	32	24	—	8
Dismissals,	20	6	—	14
Otherwise disposed of,	14	14	—	—
Pending at end of year,	17	19	—	—

Local Administration of Justice—Land Sessions. County Courts. Land Sessions. Table 68.

It appears from this table that there was a decrease of 20 in the gross number of cases for disposal from 83 in 1893 to 63 in 1894.

There have been no applications for confirmation of leases since the year 1882.

The decrees in 1894 were 24, and the dismissals 6.

In the 24 land claim cases in which there were decrees, the total amount adjudged on the decrees was £590 only in 1893, and £694 in 1894. The following table shows the distribution of the amount in the different provinces in 1893 and 1894 for comparison:— Decrees.

Provinces or Land Sessions.	Gross Amount of Decrees.		Number of Decrees.		Average Gross Sum Adjudged in each case.	
	1893.	1894.	1893.	1894.	1893.	1894.
	£	£			£	£
Total of Ireland,	590	694	32	24	19	29
Leinster,	96	182	23	19	4	10
Munster,	322	38	3	1	108	38
Ulster,	84	476	4	4	21	119
Connaught,	—	—	—	—	—	—

It appears from this table that the average gross amount awarded, without deducting allowances for set-off to landlord, for dilapidations, rent, &c., was £29, as compared with £19 in 1893, and £14 in 1892. Nineteen of the decrees were in Leinster for amounts averaging £10, one for £38 in Munster, and four for amounts averaging £119 in Ulster. In 1893 there were twenty-three decrees in Leinster, three in Munster, four in Ulster, and none in Connaught.

The total amount claimed in cases where decrees were made in 1894, was £3,921, and, as already stated, the total amount decreed was £694. In 1893 the amount claimed in cases where decrees were made (exclusive of those cases in Dublin, in which no specific sum was claimed) was £2,505, and the sum decreed was £590. Of the twenty-four cases in which decrees were obtained last year, two were in Dublin, the amount claimed being £1,679, and the amount decreed £170; sixteen in Kilkenny, the amount claimed being £167, none of which was decreed; one in Louth, the amount claimed being £100, and the amount decreed £20; one in Waterford, the amount claimed being £38, all of which was decreed; three in Antrim, the amount claimed being £1,816, and the amount decreed £416; and one in Donegal, in which the amount claimed was £200, and the amount decreed, £60.

Court of the Irish Land Commission.

Land Commission Courts. Table 69.

The Commissioners appointed under the Land Law (Ireland) Acts, 1881 and 1887, have many functions of a judicial character, therefore it is necessary in this Report to refer to the judicial portion of their proceedings, and it is convenient to do so here, as the questions dealt with are somewhat allied to those under the Act of 1870—dealt with above—and are mainly determined in the Courts of the Sub-Commissions which are thus properly dealt with as part of the local administration of justice.

PART IV. JUDICIAL STATISTICS. Land Administration: Court of Judicature—Judicial Divisions. Judicial Commission Court. Table 88.

It is unnecessary to give here a detailed account of the business of the Court of the Land Commission as the Reports of the Commissioners contain full information on the subject.

The following statement shows generally the extent and nature of the proceedings in connexion with the Court of the Land Commission during the year 1894:—

Nature of Proceedings.	Number of Cases.	Nature of Proceedings.	Number of Cases.
Applications to have fair rents fixed:—		Appeals re Fair Rents, &c.:—	
1. In court:—		Pending at beginning of year,	1,469
Pending at beginning of year,	7,512	Number lodged during 1894,	[illegible]
Entered and lodged during 1894,	[illegible]	Heard,	[illegible]
Rents fixed,	[illegible]	Withdrawn,	[illegible]
Dismissed or struck out,	[illegible]	Pending at end of year,	[illegible]
Withdrawn,	[illegible]		
Pending at end of year,	[illegible]*		
2. Out of court:—		Result of Appeals heard:†	
Agreements fixing fair rents,	[illegible]	Decisions below, affirmed,	[illegible]
Miscellaneous originating motions:—		Do. do., modified,	[illegible]
Pending at beginning of year,	[illegible]	Rents fixed below, increased,	[illegible]
Number lodged during 1894,	[illegible]	Do. do., reduced,	[illegible]
Disposed of,	[illegible]		
Pending at end of year,	[illegible]		

The following statement shows the sums of money dealt with by the Court in fixing fair rents in the year 1894:—

Fair Rents Fixed	Former Rent	Judicial Rent	Reduction: Amount	Reduction: Rate per Cent.
	£ s. d.	£ s. d.	£ s. d.	
In court,	[illegible]	[illegible]	[illegible]	[illegible]
Out of court,	[illegible]	[illegible]	[illegible]	[illegible]
Total,	[illegible]	[illegible]	[illegible]	[illegible]

From these statements it appears that during the year 1894 "fair rents" were fixed in [illegible] cases ([illegible] in court and [illegible] out of court), the "former rent" of the holdings dealt with in these cases being in round numbers £[illegible] and the "judicial rent" sanctioned by the Court £[illegible], showing a reduction of £[illegible], or [illegible] per cent. of the "former rent." Some of the "judicial rents" included in the above are liable to variation on appeal.

The number of cases of appeal from the Land Court to the Court of Appeal, and how these were disposed of, will be found in Table [illegible] of Appendix, and are referred to at page [illegible] under the head of Appellate Jurisdiction.

Purchase of Land. Tables 93 and 94.

A Return of Sales to Tenants under the Purchase of Land (Ireland) Act, 1885, in which the Loans were issued from the 22nd August, 1885, to the 31st December, 1894, has been furnished by the Commissioners, and is given in Table 93, page [illegible].

* See Note at foot of Table [illegible], page [illegible].
† The numbers here given refer to actual cases, cross appeals being counted as one.

From this Return and those published in the Reports on Criminal and Judicial Statistics for the seven years 1887–93, we learn that the number of Tenant Purchasers in the first year (August, 1885—August, 1886), in which the Act was in operation, was 1,294; in the second 2,516, in the third 4,470, in the fourth 3,819, in the fifth 2,708, in the sixth 3,067, in the seventh 3,378, in the eighth 3,387, in the period from 22nd August, 1893, to the 31st December, 1893, 306, and in the (calendar) year ended 31st December last, 1,249; the total number up to the last mentioned date being 24,879, of whom 12,883, or 51·8 per cent., were in Ulster; 4,346, or 17·5 per cent., in Munster; 2,486, or 10·0 per cent., in Leinster; and 5,164, or 20·7 per cent., in Connaught. The total Purchase-money for the whole period, from the 22nd August, 1885, to the 31st December, 1894, was £10,025,710, of which £425,800 was for Sales in the year ended 31st December, 1894, and the total amount of Loans £9,861,244, including £422,804 advanced during last year. In the first year the average number of years' Purchase on Net Rental was 18·3, in the second 17·3, in the third 17·4, in the fourth 17·2, in the fifth 16·2, in the sixth 16·6, in the seventh 16·9, in the eighth 17·1; in the period from 22nd August, 1893, to 31st December of that year, 16·6; and in the year ended 31st December last, 15·9.

Table 94, on page 162, contains a Return of Sales to Tenants under the Purchase of Land (Ireland) Act, 1891, in which Loans were issued during the year ending the 31st December, 1894. These Loans amounted to £787,897, the Purchase-money agreed upon being £802,186; in the year 1892 (the first in which Loans were issued under the Act), the amount lent was £90,443, and the Purchase-money agreed upon £95,149; and in the year 1893 the loans were £646,516, and the Purchase-money £684,878. In the three years combined the Purchase-money amounted to £1,582,172, and the Loans to £1,524,391. The Loans for the three years were made to 4,509 Tenant purchasers, of whom 1,950, or 43 per cent., were in Ulster; 1,103, or 25 per cent., in Munster; 729, or 16 per cent., in Leinster; and 727, or 16 per cent., in Connaught. The average number of years' Purchase on the Net Rental was 17·0 in each of the two years 1892–3, and 16·9 in 1894.

Proceedings of Sheriffs.

The proceedings of Sheriffs in the year of their office 1894–95, including those having relation to Jurors summoned, and those already referred to, are set forth in detail in Tables 87 and 89.

Jurors.

The revision of the General Jurors' Lists resulted in the striking off of 48,480 out of 120,650 persons, or 40 per cent.; there were only 253 persons added by Revision Court, including 234 in the City of Dublin.

Besides those struck off on revision there were 344 exempted by Clerks of the Peace, and 3 struck off by Judges. This gives the total number of Jurors on the corrected General Jurors' Books (when handed to the Sheriffs) in all Ireland as 72,438, of whom 61,080 were on rated qualification, 7,614 were £10 freeholders, 3,143 were £50 lease-holders, 574 Directors or Managers of Public Companies, and 28 Harbour Commissioners.

In the case of 16,570 persons on the Special Jurors' Lists, 5,392 persons were struck off by Revision Court, and 213 exempted by the Clerks of the Peace; 173 were added by Revision Court, so that there was a net reduction of 5,242, or 32 per cent. When handed to the Sheriffs the books showed 11,328 Special Jurors.

The total number of jurors returned as summoned in the year is 48,116, as compared with 47,593 in 1893. Of the number for 1894, 3,420 were Grand

Part II. Irish Land Acts. Land Judicature Commissioners. [illegible] Land Commission Court. Purchase of Land. Tables 93 and 94. Proceedings of Sheriffs. Revision of Jurors' Lists and corrections of Jurors' Books. Tables 88. Jurors summoned. Table 89.

Jurors* for Assizes, Commissions, and Superior Courts; 3,882 were Grand Jurors for Quarter Sessions; 3,630* were Special Jurors for Assizes, Commissions, and Superior Courts; 15,881 were Petit and Common Jurors for Assizes, Commissions, and Superior Courts; 14,821 were Petit Jurors for Quarter Sessions; 1,699 were Jurors in Civil Bill cases before County Court Judges or Recorders; and 821 were Jurors for other purposes.

In the following summary the statistics of appeals at Quarter Sessions are compared with the figures for 1893:—

Appeals from Magistrates to Quarter Sessions. Table 91.

Appeals at Quarter Sessions.	1894.	1893.	Increase, 1894.	Decrease, 1894.
Appeals from Magistrates:—				
Affirmed,	337	366	—	53
Reversed,	131	167	—	58
Varied,	80	73	13	—
Otherwise disposed of (including cases where there was no appearance),	130	104	—	18
Total,	742	650	—	103

The number of appeals from Magistrates heard at Quarter Sessions, as appears from the above figures, was 98 fewer in 1894 than in 1893, the number for which year was 79 under that for 1892. Of the appeals heard and decided in Court during 1894, in 289 cases the previous decisions were affirmed, in 167 reversed, and in 79 varied.

Spirit Licences.

Spirit Licences.

The number of licences granted at other Quarter Sessions than the annual licensing Sessions was 815 which, with the number granted or confirmed at the Annual Sessions (1,701), makes 2,517 in all; and of these 484 were on original application, compared with 493 in 1893.

SMALLER DISTRICT ADMINISTRATION OF JUSTICE.

Local Charter Courts.

Local Charter Courts. — Table 91.

The following summary shows the business in 1894 in the eight Local Charter Courts, viz. :—Clonmel Court of Conscience, Drogheda Court of Conscience, Dublin Lord Mayor's Court (see note (*) page 160), Dublin Court of Conscience, Kilkenny Court of Conscience, Limerick Court of Conscience, Londonderry Court of Conscience, and Wexford Court of Conscience. There were summonses issued, 4,244, being 275 under the number for 1893; causes heard, 3,374; decisions for plaintiff, 2,813; for defendant, 190; otherwise disposed of, 371.

Petty Sessions Courts.

Petty Sessions Courts. — Table 92. Civil proceedings.

Table 92 in the Appendix shows the civil business at the Courts of Petty Sessions. The summonses issued were 117,827, which shows a decrease of 14,815 as compared with the number in 1893, following a decrease of 672 in 1893 as compared with 1892.

Civil cases at Petty Sessions other than proceedings against owners and weekly tenants were disposed of as follows :—

The table also shows the proceedings relating to cottier tenants under the Landlord and Tenant Act, 1860 (Stat. 23 & 24 Vic., c. 154), under which cottier tenements of less than half an acre, under £5 rent, and repaired by landlord, may be summarily recovered at Petty Sessions, for waste, for non-payment of rent, or for overholding. The cases for summary recovery of tenements in towns against weekly tenants, under Stat. 14 & 15 Vic., c. 92, sec. 15, are also shown.

PART II. JUDICIAL STATISTICS. Local Administration of Justice—Smaller Districts. Petty Sessions Courts.

The proceedings against cottier and weekly tenants, and against servants, herdsmen, and caretakers in 1894, appear from the returns to have been as follows:—

Proceedings against Cottier and Weekly Tenants. Table 20.

Summary Recovery of Possession.	Summonses Issued.	Complaints Heard.	Warrants to Special Bailiffs.	Cases in which Decree not executed.
Cottier Tenants. Under Stat. 23 & 24 Vic., c. 154.				
For Waste (sec. 84),	78	16		
For Non-payment of Rent (sec. 85),	338	289		
Caretakers, Servants, and Cottier Tenants.				
For Overholding (sec. 86),	2,047	1,677	1,697	81
Weekly Tenants. Under Stat. 14 & 15 Vic., c. 92.				
For Overholding in Towns (sec. 15),	28,838	19,126	22,098	32
Total,	31,330	20,941	23,895	113

The returns further indicate the number of occasions on which, in consequence of the non-attendance of Magistrates, Petty Sessions were not held. This number (390), as compared with 13,194 sittings of Petty Sessions Courts other than Dublin Police Courts, gives a proportion of 3·0 per cent.; but this proportion is differently distributed, and reaches 5·4 per cent. in the province of Connaught, as appears from the following table:—

Non-attendance of Magistrates. Table 20.

Provinces.	Number of occasions on which, through non-attendance of Magistrates, Petty Sessions were not held.	Number of other Petty Sessions' sittings.	Percentage of occasions when sittings not held to number of sittings held.
			Per cent.
Leinster, (127 Courts),	83	3,215*	2·6
Munster, (148 ,,),	109	4,166	2·6
Ulster, (169 ,,),	81	3,932	2·0
Connaught, (118 ,,),	117	2,093	5·4
Total, (562 Courts),*	390	13,194*	3·0

* Not including 796 sittings of 4 Metropolitan Police District Courts at which local Magistrates attend.

In all the provinces the postponements were less frequent than they were during the preceding year, the returns for which showed a marked improvement as compared with those for 1892. In Leinster the postponements fell from 99 in 1893 to 83 last year; in Munster the number declined from 132 to 109; in Ulster there was a decrease from 88 to 81; and in Connaught the number fell from 140 to 117. The decrease for all Ireland was 69.

[illegible]

IRELAND.

[illegible]

Part I.

383

PART IV.—EFFECTIVE STRENGTH OF THE FORCE, IN DIVISIONS, ON 31ST MARCH, [illegible]

Divisions.	[illegible]	Inspectors.	Sergeants.	Constables.	Detective Officers.	Total Effective Strength, [illegible]	Population according to Census of [illegible]	Number of Effective Strength per [illegible] of Population.
1 A, City, S.W.	[illegible]	[illegible]	[illegible]	[illegible]	—	[illegible]	[illegible]	[illegible]
2 B, " S.E.	[illegible]	[illegible]	[illegible]	[illegible]	—	[illegible]	[illegible]	[illegible]
3 C, " N.E.	[illegible]	[illegible]	[illegible]	[illegible]	—	[illegible]	[illegible]	[illegible]
4 D, " N.W. and Rural*	[illegible]	[illegible]	[illegible]	[illegible]	—	[illegible]	[illegible]	[illegible]
5 E, " E. and Rural†	[illegible]	[illegible]	[illegible]	[illegible]	—	[illegible]	[illegible]	[illegible]
6 F, Rural‡	[illegible]	[illegible]	[illegible]	[illegible]	—	[illegible]	[illegible]	[illegible]
7 G.§	[illegible]	[illegible]	[illegible]	[illegible]	10	[illegible]	—	—
Total	[illegible]	[illegible]	[illegible]	[illegible]	[illegible]	[illegible]	[illegible]	[illegible]

* D, Rural part.—[illegible]

† E, Rural part.—[illegible]

‡ F, Rural.—[illegible]

§ The Officers and Constables of the G Division are employed as "Detectives."

[illegible] employed in Government Departments and on private service with Public Bodies.

[illegible] (and [illegible]) ... the Year ended 31st December, 1854.

[illegible]	[illegible]
Leinster.	
Dublin	[illegible]
Drogheda, Town of	[illegible]
Dublin County	[illegible]
Dublin City (exclusive of County) ... Police District	
A.	[illegible]
B.	[illegible]
C.	[illegible]
D.	[illegible]
E.	[illegible]
F.	[illegible]
Total of New Police District	[illegible]
Kildare	[illegible]
Kilkenny	[illegible]
King's County	[illegible]
Longford	[illegible]
Louth	[illegible]
Meath	[illegible]
Queen's County	[illegible]
Westmeath	[illegible]
Wexford	[illegible]
Wicklow	[illegible]
Total in Province	[illegible]
Munster.	
Clare	[illegible]
Cork, East Riding	[illegible]

NATURE OF OFFENCE.

Class 1.—Offences against the Person.

[illegible]

Total of No. 1.

Class 2.—Offences against Property with Violence.

[illegible]

Total of No. 2.

Class 3.—Offences against Property without Violence.

[illegible]

Total of No. 3.

Class 4.—Malicious Offences against Property.

[illegible]

Total of No. 4.

Class 5.—Forgery and Offences against the Currency.

[illegible]

[illegible]

[illegible]
[illegible]
Total of No. 1.
[illegible]
Total of No. 2.
[illegible]
Total of No. 3.
[illegible]
Total of No. 4.
[illegible]
Total of No. 5.
[illegible]
Total of No. 6.
General Total.

[illegible]

[illegible]

TABLE [illegible]

DETERMINED SUMMARILY.

Cork City,	[illegible]
Kerry,	[illegible]
Limerick,	[illegible]
Limerick City,	[illegible]
Tipperary, North Riding,	[illegible]
Tipperary, South Riding,	[illegible]
Waterford,	[illegible]
Waterford City,	[illegible]
Total of Province,	[illegible]
ULSTER:	
Antrim,	[illegible]
Armagh,	[illegible]
Belfast, City of,	[illegible]
Carrickfergus, Town of,	[illegible]
Cavan,	[illegible]
Donegal,	[illegible]
Down,	[illegible]
Fermanagh,	[illegible]
Londonderry,	[illegible]
Monaghan,	[illegible]
Tyrone,	[illegible]
Total of Province,	[illegible]
CONNAUGHT:	
Galway, East Riding,	[illegible]
Galway, West Riding,	[illegible]
Galway, Town of,	[illegible]
Leitrim,	[illegible]
Mayo,	[illegible]
Roscommon,	[illegible]
Sligo,	[illegible]
Total of Province,	[illegible]
Total of Ireland,	[illegible]

[illegible]

[illegible]	[illegible]	[illegible]	[illegible]	Total.
Leinster:				
Carlow,	[illegible]	[illegible]	[illegible]	[illegible]
Drogheda, Town of,	[illegible]	[illegible]	[illegible]	[illegible]
Dublin County (rural),	[illegible]	[illegible]	[illegible]	[illegible]
Dublin City and part of County [illegible]				
A.,	[illegible]	[illegible]	[illegible]	[illegible]
B.,	[illegible]	[illegible]	[illegible]	[illegible]
C.,	[illegible]	[illegible]	[illegible]	[illegible]
D.,	[illegible]	[illegible]	[illegible]	[illegible]
E.,	[illegible]	[illegible]	[illegible]	[illegible]
F.,	[illegible]	[illegible]	[illegible]	[illegible]
Total of Dublin City,	[illegible]	[illegible]	[illegible]	[illegible]
Kildare,	[illegible]	[illegible]	[illegible]	[illegible]
Kilkenny,	[illegible]	[illegible]	[illegible]	[illegible]
King's County,	[illegible]	[illegible]	[illegible]	[illegible]
Longford,	[illegible]	[illegible]	[illegible]	[illegible]
Louth,	[illegible]	[illegible]	[illegible]	[illegible]
Meath,	[illegible]	[illegible]	[illegible]	[illegible]
Queen's County,	[illegible]	[illegible]	[illegible]	[illegible]
Westmeath,	[illegible]	[illegible]	[illegible]	[illegible]
Wexford,	[illegible]	[illegible]	[illegible]	[illegible]
Wicklow,	[illegible]	[illegible]	[illegible]	[illegible]
Total of Province,	[illegible]	[illegible]	[illegible]	[illegible]
Munster:				
Clare,	[illegible]	[illegible]	[illegible]	[illegible]
Cork, East Riding,	[illegible]	[illegible]	[illegible]	[illegible]
Cork, West Riding,	[illegible]	[illegible]	[illegible]	[illegible]
Cork City,	[illegible]	[illegible]	[illegible]	[illegible]
Kerry,	[illegible]	[illegible]	[illegible]	[illegible]
Limerick,	[illegible]	[illegible]	[illegible]	[illegible]
Munster, continued:				
Limerick City,	[illegible]	[illegible]	[illegible]	[illegible]
Tipperary, North Riding,	[illegible]	[illegible]	[illegible]	[illegible]
Tipperary, South Riding,	[illegible]	[illegible]	[illegible]	[illegible]
Waterford,	[illegible]	[illegible]	[illegible]	[illegible]
Waterford City,	[illegible]	[illegible]	[illegible]	[illegible]
Total of Province,	[illegible]	[illegible]	[illegible]	[illegible]
Ulster:				
Antrim,	[illegible]	[illegible]	[illegible]	[illegible]
Armagh,	[illegible]	[illegible]	[illegible]	[illegible]
Belfast, City of,	[illegible]	[illegible]	[illegible]	[illegible]
Carrickfergus, Town of,	[illegible]	[illegible]	[illegible]	[illegible]
Cavan,	[illegible]	[illegible]	[illegible]	[illegible]
Donegal,	[illegible]	[illegible]	[illegible]	[illegible]
Down,	[illegible]	[illegible]	[illegible]	[illegible]
Fermanagh,	[illegible]	[illegible]	[illegible]	[illegible]
Londonderry,	[illegible]	[illegible]	[illegible]	[illegible]
Monaghan,	[illegible]	[illegible]	[illegible]	[illegible]
Tyrone,	[illegible]	[illegible]	[illegible]	[illegible]
Total of Province,	[illegible]	[illegible]	[illegible]	[illegible]
Connaught:				
Galway, East Riding,	[illegible]	[illegible]	[illegible]	[illegible]
Galway, West Riding,	[illegible]	[illegible]	[illegible]	[illegible]
Galway, Town,	[illegible]	[illegible]	[illegible]	[illegible]
Leitrim,	[illegible]	[illegible]	[illegible]	[illegible]
Mayo,	[illegible]	[illegible]	[illegible]	[illegible]
Roscommon,	[illegible]	[illegible]	[illegible]	[illegible]
Sligo,	[illegible]	[illegible]	[illegible]	[illegible]
Total of Province,	[illegible]	[illegible]	[illegible]	[illegible]
Total of Ireland,	[illegible]	[illegible]	[illegible]	[illegible]

TABLES SHOWING DISTRICTS PROCLAIMED.

TABLE 10.—RETURN showing the several DISTRICTS which were subject to PROCLAMATIONS in force under [illegible] WM. IV., CAP. [illegible], on the [illegible] December, [illegible].

County.	Proclaimed District.	Date of Proclamation.
[illegible]	The County	[illegible]
[illegible]	"	[illegible]
[illegible]	"	[illegible]
[illegible]	"	[illegible]
[illegible]	"	[illegible]

(a) [illegible]

THE PEACE PRESERVATION (IRELAND) ACT, [illegible], [illegible] PEACE PRESERVATION (IRELAND) CONTINUANCE ACT, [illegible], the CRIMINAL LAW AND PROCEDURE (IRELAND) ACT, [illegible], and the EXPIRING LAWS CONTINUANCE ACTS.

TABLE 11.—RETURN [illegible] showing the several DISTRICTS which were under the operation of PROCLAMATIONS [illegible] on the [illegible] December, [illegible].

County, &c.	Proclaimed District.	Date of Proclamation.
Armagh	The Baronies of [illegible]	[illegible]
Belfast	The Borough	[illegible]
[illegible]	The County	[illegible]
[illegible]	"	[illegible]
[illegible]	"	[illegible]
Cork City	The County of the City	[illegible]
[illegible]	The [illegible] and the Parishes of [illegible]	[illegible]
[illegible]	The County of the Town	[illegible]
[illegible]	The County	[illegible]
Dublin City	The Metropolitan Police District	[illegible]
Galway	The County	[illegible]
Galway Town	The County of the Town	[illegible]
[illegible]	The County	[illegible]
[illegible]	"	[illegible]
Kilkenny	"	[illegible]
[illegible]	"	[illegible]
[illegible]	"	[illegible]
[illegible]	"	[illegible]
Limerick City	The County of the City	[illegible]
Londonderry City	The Borough	[illegible]
Longford	The County	[illegible]
Mayo	"	[illegible]
Meath	"	[illegible]
Monaghan	[illegible]	[illegible]
[illegible]	The County	[illegible]
[illegible]	"	[illegible]
Sligo	"	[illegible]
Tipperary	"	[illegible]
Waterford	"	[illegible]
Waterford City	The County of the City	[illegible]
Westmeath	The County	[illegible]
Wexford	"	[illegible]

(a) [illegible]
(b) [illegible]
(c) [illegible]

TABLE 14.—RETURN No. III., showing the several DISTRICTS which were under the operation of PROCLAMATION IN COUNCIL under the above Act, prohibiting the CARRYING OF ARMS, &c., on the 31st December, 1884.

County, &c.	Proclaimed Districts.	Date of Proclamation.
Armagh	That part of the Parish of Newry in which is situate that portion of the town of Newry which is in the County Armagh, and also that part of the Barony of Lower Orior which is contiguous to the aforesaid part of the Parish of Newry.	27 November, [illegible]
Cavan	The County.	3 April, [illegible]
Down	The Barony or Lordship of Newry.	27 November, [illegible]
Fermanagh	The County.	19 December, [illegible]
Monaghan	The County (a)	5 April, [illegible]
Tyrone	The Baronies of Dungannon Upper and Middle.	29 May, [illegible]
	The Baronies of Omagh East, Omagh West, and Clogher.	19 December, [illegible]

(a) The Baronies of Farney and Cremorne and the Parish of [illegible] proclaimed for having or carrying Arms, &c., on [illegible].

TABLE 15.—STATE PRISONS.—CLASSIFICATION of ORDINARY CRIMINALS Committed during the year 1884, [illegible] by General Prisons Board.

[illegible]	[illegible]		[illegible]		[illegible]																								[illegible]	
	M.	F.	M.	F.	M.	F.	M.	F.	M.	F.	M.	F.	M.	F.	M.	F.	M.	F.	M.	F.	M.	F.	M.	F.	M.	F.	M.	F.	M.	F.
[illegible]	[illegible]	[illegible]	[illegible]	[illegible]	[illegible]	[illegible]	[illegible]	[illegible]	[illegible]	[illegible]	[illegible]	[illegible]	[illegible]	[illegible]	[illegible]	[illegible]	[illegible]	[illegible]	[illegible]	[illegible]	[illegible]	[illegible]	[illegible]	[illegible]	[illegible]	[illegible]	[illegible]	[illegible]	[illegible]	[illegible]

[illegible]	[illegible]		[illegible]		[illegible]		[illegible]		[illegible]		[illegible]		[illegible]		[illegible]		[illegible]	
	M.	F.	M.	F.	M.	F.	M.	F.	M.	F.	M.	F.	M.	F.	M.	F.	M.	F.
[illegible]	[illegible]	[illegible]	[illegible]	[illegible]	[illegible]	[illegible]	[illegible]	[illegible]	[illegible]	[illegible]	[illegible]	[illegible]	[illegible]	[illegible]	[illegible]	[illegible]	[illegible]	[illegible]

TABLE [illegible].—STATE PRISONS.—CLASSIFICATION of ORDINARY CRIMINALS Committed during the Year [illegible], received by General Prison Boards—continued.

(3) AS TO BIRTHPLACE.	[illegible]						[illegible]						[illegible]						[illegible]						[illegible]						[illegible]						[illegible]					
	M.	W.	M.	W.	M.	W.	M.	W.	M.	W.	M.	W.	M.	W.	M.	W.	M.	W.	M.	W.	M.	W.	M.	W.	M.	W.	M.	W.	M.	W.	M.	W.	M.	W.	M.	W.	M.	W.	M.	W.	M.	W.
Number in all Larger District Prisons.	[illegible]	[illegible]	[illegible]	[illegible]	[illegible]	[illegible]	[illegible]	[illegible]	[illegible]	[illegible]	[illegible]	[illegible]	[illegible]	[illegible]	[illegible]	[illegible]	[illegible]	[illegible]	[illegible]	[illegible]	[illegible]	[illegible]	[illegible]	[illegible]	[illegible]	[illegible]	[illegible]	[illegible]	[illegible]	[illegible]	[illegible]	[illegible]	[illegible]	[illegible]	[illegible]	[illegible]	[illegible]	[illegible]	[illegible]	[illegible]	[illegible]	[illegible]

(4) AS TO DEGREES OF INSTRUCTION.	[illegible]		[illegible]		[illegible]		[illegible]		[illegible]	
	M.	W.	M.	W.	M.	W.	M.	W.	M.	W.
Number in all Larger District Prisons.	[illegible]	[illegible]	[illegible]	[illegible]	[illegible]	[illegible]	[illegible]	[illegible]	[illegible]	[illegible]

TABLE [illegible] in [illegible] at the end of [illegible], with the number [illegible] in [illegible].

[illegible]		[illegible]		[illegible]	
[illegible]	[illegible]	[illegible]	[illegible]	[illegible]	[illegible]
[illegible]	Cavan.	[illegible]		66	[illegible]
[illegible]	Mayo.	[illegible]		[illegible]	[illegible]
[illegible]	Galway.	[illegible]		[illegible]	[illegible]
[illegible]	Clare.	[illegible]		[illegible]	[illegible]
[illegible]	Kerry.			[illegible]	[illegible]
[illegible]	Kilkenny.	[illegible]		[illegible]	[illegible]
[illegible]	Cork.	[illegible]		[illegible]	[illegible]
[illegible]	Clare.			[illegible]	[illegible]
[illegible]	Donegal.			[illegible]	[illegible]
[illegible]	Galway.	[illegible]		[illegible]	[illegible]
[illegible]	Dublin.	[illegible]		[illegible]	[illegible]
[illegible]	Waterford.			[illegible]	[illegible]
[illegible]	[illegible]	[illegible]		[illegible]	[illegible]
[illegible]	[illegible]	[illegible]		[illegible]	[illegible]
[illegible]	[illegible]	[illegible]		[illegible]	[illegible]
[illegible]	Cork.			[illegible]	
Total.		[illegible]		[illegible]	[illegible]

(b) [illegible] in [illegible] at the end of [illegible], with the number [illegible] in [illegible].

[illegible]	[illegible]		[illegible]	
	[illegible]	[illegible]	[illegible]	[illegible]
[illegible]	[illegible]	[illegible]	[illegible]	[illegible]

TABLE [illegible]. [illegible] AND COST OF [illegible] IN THE YEAR [illegible] [illegible]

[illegible]

[illegible]

[illegible]

[illegible]

[illegible]

[illegible]

TABLE 14.—continued.—CRIMINAL PROCEEDINGS AT ASSIZES, COMMISSION, AND QUARTER SESSIONS,— and the RESULT of the PROCEEDINGS—[illegible] Returns.

OFFENCES.	SENTENCES.											
[illegible]	[illegible]										[illegible]	
	[illegible]		[illegible]		[illegible]		[illegible]		[illegible]		[illegible]	
	M.	F.	M.	F.	M.	F.	M.	F.	M.	F.	M.	F.
[illegible]	[illegible]	[illegible]	[illegible]	[illegible]	[illegible]	[illegible]	[illegible]	[illegible]	[illegible]	[illegible]	[illegible]	[illegible]
Total of No. 1.	[illegible]	[illegible]	[illegible]	[illegible]	[illegible]	[illegible]	[illegible]	[illegible]	[illegible]	[illegible]	[illegible]	[illegible]
[illegible]	[illegible]	[illegible]	[illegible]	[illegible]	[illegible]	[illegible]	[illegible]	[illegible]	[illegible]	[illegible]	[illegible]	[illegible]
Total of No. 2.	[illegible]	[illegible]	[illegible]	[illegible]	[illegible]	[illegible]	[illegible]	[illegible]	[illegible]	[illegible]	[illegible]	[illegible]
[illegible]	[illegible]	[illegible]	[illegible]	[illegible]	[illegible]	[illegible]	[illegible]	[illegible]	[illegible]	[illegible]	[illegible]	[illegible]
Total of No. 3.	[illegible]	[illegible]	[illegible]	[illegible]	[illegible]	[illegible]	[illegible]	[illegible]	[illegible]	[illegible]	[illegible]	[illegible]
[illegible]	[illegible]	[illegible]	[illegible]	[illegible]	[illegible]	[illegible]	[illegible]	[illegible]	[illegible]	[illegible]	[illegible]	[illegible]
Total of No. 4.	[illegible]	[illegible]	[illegible]	[illegible]	[illegible]	[illegible]	[illegible]	[illegible]	[illegible]	[illegible]	[illegible]	[illegible]
[illegible]	[illegible]	[illegible]	[illegible]	[illegible]	[illegible]	[illegible]	[illegible]	[illegible]	[illegible]	[illegible]	[illegible]	[illegible]
Total of No. 5.	[illegible]	[illegible]	[illegible]	[illegible]	[illegible]	[illegible]	[illegible]	[illegible]	[illegible]	[illegible]	[illegible]	[illegible]
[illegible]	[illegible]	[illegible]	[illegible]	[illegible]	[illegible]	[illegible]	[illegible]	[illegible]	[illegible]	[illegible]	[illegible]	[illegible]

[illegible]	[illegible]	[illegible]	[illegible]	[illegible]	[illegible]	OFFENCES. [illegible]
[illegible]	[illegible]	[illegible]	[illegible]	[illegible]	[illegible]	No. 1.—Offences against the Person. [illegible]
[illegible]	[illegible]	[illegible]	[illegible]	[illegible]	[illegible]	Total of No. 1.
[illegible]	[illegible]	[illegible]	[illegible]	[illegible]	[illegible]	No. 2.—Offences against Property, with Violence. [illegible]
[illegible]	[illegible]	[illegible]	[illegible]	[illegible]	[illegible]	Total of No. 2.
[illegible]	[illegible]	[illegible]	[illegible]	[illegible]	[illegible]	No. 3.—Offences against Property, without Violence. [illegible]
[illegible]	[illegible]	[illegible]	[illegible]	[illegible]	[illegible]	Total of No. 3.
[illegible]	[illegible]	[illegible]	[illegible]	[illegible]	[illegible]	No. 4.—Malicious Offences against Property. [illegible]
[illegible]	[illegible]	[illegible]	[illegible]	[illegible]	[illegible]	Total of No. 4.
[illegible]	[illegible]	[illegible]	[illegible]	[illegible]	[illegible]	No. 5.—Forgery and Offences against the Currency. [illegible]
[illegible]	[illegible]	[illegible]	[illegible]	[illegible]	[illegible]	Total of No. 5.
[illegible]	[illegible]	[illegible]	[illegible]	[illegible]	[illegible]	No. 6.—Offences not included in the above Classes. [illegible]
[illegible]	[illegible]	[illegible]	[illegible]	[illegible]	[illegible]	Total of No. 6.
[illegible]	[illegible]	[illegible]	[illegible]	[illegible]	[illegible]	GRAND TOTAL.

[illegible]	[illegible]	[illegible]	[illegible]	.	—	[illegible]	Cavan.
[illegible]	[illegible]	[illegible]	[illegible]	.	—	[illegible]	Clare.
[illegible]	[illegible]	[illegible]	[illegible]	.	—	[illegible]	Cork County.
[illegible]	[illegible]	[illegible]	[illegible]	.	—		Cork City.
[illegible]	[illegible]	[illegible]	[illegible]	.	—	[illegible]	Donegal.
[illegible]	[illegible]	[illegible]	[illegible]	.	—	[illegible]	Down.
[illegible]	[illegible]	[illegible]	[illegible]	.	—	[illegible]	Drogheda Town.
[illegible]	[illegible]	[illegible]	[illegible]	.	—	[illegible]	Dublin County.
[illegible]	[illegible]	[illegible]	[illegible]	.	—		Dublin City.
[illegible]	[illegible]	[illegible]	[illegible]	.	—	[illegible]	Fermanagh.
[illegible]	[illegible]		—	.	—	[illegible]	Galway County.
[illegible]	[illegible]	[illegible]	[illegible]	.	—		Galway Town.
[illegible]	[illegible]		—	.	—	[illegible]	Kerry.
[illegible]	[illegible]	[illegible]	[illegible]	.	—	[illegible]	Kildare.
[illegible]	[illegible]	[illegible]	[illegible]	.	—	[illegible]	Kilkenny County.
[illegible]	[illegible]	[illegible]	[illegible]	.	—		Kilkenny City.
[illegible]	[illegible]	[illegible]	[illegible]	.	—	[illegible]	King's County.
[illegible]	[illegible]	[illegible]	[illegible]	.	—	[illegible]	Leitrim.
[illegible]	[illegible]	[illegible]	[illegible]	.	—	[illegible]	Limerick County.
[illegible]	[illegible]	[illegible]	[illegible]	.	—		Limerick City.
[illegible]	[illegible]	[illegible]	[illegible]	.	—	[illegible]	Londonderry.
[illegible]	[illegible]		—	.	—	[illegible]	Longford.
[illegible]	[illegible]	[illegible]	[illegible]	.	—	[illegible]	Louth.
[illegible]	[illegible]		—	.	—	[illegible]	Mayo.
[illegible]	[illegible]	[illegible]	[illegible]	.	—	[illegible]	Meath.
[illegible]	[illegible]	[illegible]	[illegible]	.	—	[illegible]	Monaghan.
[illegible]	[illegible]	[illegible]	[illegible]	.	—	[illegible]	Queen's County.
[illegible]	[illegible]		—	.	—	[illegible]	Roscommon.
[illegible]	[illegible]		—	.	—	[illegible]	Sligo.
[illegible]	[illegible]	[illegible]	[illegible]	.	—	[illegible]	Tipperary, North Ri[illegible]
[illegible]	[illegible]	[illegible]	[illegible]	.	—		Tipperary, South Ri[illegible]
[illegible]	[illegible]		—	.	—	[illegible]	Tyrone.
[illegible]	[illegible]	[illegible]	[illegible]	.	—	[illegible]	Waterford County.
	[illegible]	[illegible]	[illegible]	.	—		Waterford City.

[illegible]					[illegible]			[illegible]	[illegible]							
[illegible]	[illegible]	[illegible]	[illegible]	[illegible]	[illegible]	[illegible]	[illegible] and [illegible]		[illegible]	[illegible]	[illegible]	[illegible]	[illegible]	[illegible]	[illegible]
[illegible]	[illegible]	[illegible]	[illegible]	[illegible]	[illegible]	[illegible]	[illegible]	[illegible]	[illegible]	[illegible]	[illegible]	[illegible]	[illegible]			[illegible]
[illegible]	[illegible]	[illegible]	[illegible]	[illegible]	[illegible]	[illegible]	[illegible]	[illegible]	[illegible]	[illegible]	[illegible]	[illegible]	[illegible]	[illegible]		[illegible]
[illegible]	[illegible]	[illegible]	[illegible]	[illegible]	[illegible]	[illegible]	[illegible]	[illegible]	[illegible]	[illegible]	[illegible]	[illegible]	[illegible]			[illegible]
[illegible]	[illegible]	[illegible]	[illegible]		[illegible]	[illegible]	[illegible]	[illegible]	[illegible]	11	[illegible]	[illegible]	[illegible]			[illegible]

[illegible]

[illegible]	[illegible]	[illegible]	[illegible]	[illegible]
[illegible]	[illegible]	[illegible]	[illegible]	[illegible]

[illegible]

[illegible]

[illegible]	[illegible]	[illegible]	[illegible]	[illegible]	[illegible]	[illegible]	[illegible]
[illegible]	[illegible]	[illegible]	[illegible]	[illegible]	[illegible]	[illegible]	[illegible]

IRELAND.

[illegible]	Total			[illegible]		[illegible]		[illegible]		[illegible]		[illegible]		[illegible]	
[illegible]	[illegible]	[illegible]	[illegible]	[illegible]	[illegible]	[illegible]	[illegible]	[illegible]	[illegible]	[illegible]	[illegible]	[illegible]	[illegible]	[illegible]	[illegible]	[illegible]	[illegible]
[illegible] during the year 1884.	[illegible]	[illegible]	[illegible]	[illegible]	[illegible]	[illegible]	[illegible]	[illegible]	[illegible]	[illegible]	[illegible]	[illegible]	[illegible]	[illegible]	[illegible]	[illegible]	[illegible]

[illegible]

[illegible]

[illegible]

[illegible]

O 2

[illegible]

[illegible]	[illegible]	[illegible]	[illegible]	[illegible]	[illegible]	Stock
[illegible]	[illegible]	[illegible]	[illegible]	[illegible]	[illegible]	[illegible]
Total	[illegible]	[illegible]	[illegible]	[illegible]	[illegible]	[illegible]

[illegible]

[illegible]

12. [illegible]

TABLE [illegible].—HIGH COURT OF JUSTICE—CHANCERY DIVISION.—Return of Proceedings in the Office of the Lord Chancellor's Secretary, made by the Lord Chancellor's Secretary, and in the Office of the Secretary at the Rolls, made by the Secretary at the Rolls, in the Year [illegible].

[illegible]

TABLE [illegible].—HIGH COURT OF JUSTICE—CHANCERY DIVISION.—RETURN of PROCEEDINGS in the CROWN and [illegible] OFFICE for the Year [illegible], made by the Clerk of the Crown and [illegible].

[illegible]

[illegible]

PROCEEDINGS	Number	PROCEEDINGS	Number
[illegible]	[illegible]	[illegible]	[illegible]

[illegible]

TABLE 2.—HIGH COURT OF JUSTICE.—CHANCERY DIVISION.—LAND JUDGE.

[illegible]

PROCEEDINGS	Number	PROCEEDINGS	Number
[illegible]	[illegible]	[illegible]	[illegible]

[illegible]

PROCEEDINGS	Number	PROCEEDINGS	Number
[illegible]	[illegible]	[illegible]	[illegible]

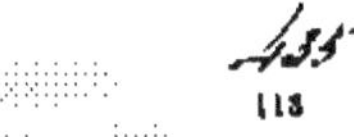

TABLE [illegible].—EXCHEQUER DIVISION.—[illegible]

[illegible]

TABLE [illegible].—[illegible] EXCHEQUER DIVISION[illegible]

[illegible]

TABLE [illegible].—[illegible] EXCHEQUER DIVISION[illegible]

[illegible]

IRELAND.

TABLE [illegible].—HIGH COURT OF JUSTICE, QUEEN'S BENCH DIVISION, CROWN SIDE.—(a) Proceedings other than Cases entered for Jury Trial.—[illegible]

[illegible]

[illegible]	[illegible]	[illegible]	[illegible]		[illegible]	[illegible]	[illegible]	[illegible]
			[illegible]	[illegible]				
	None.						£ s. d.	£ s. d.

[illegible]

[illegible]

[illegible]

[illegible]

TABLE [illegible].—HIGH COURT OF JUSTICE—CHANCERY DIVISION—LAND JUDGES.—(a.) RETURN of PROCEEDINGS in the LOCAL REGISTRATION of TITLE (IRELAND) OFFICE for the Year 1894, made by the Registrar.

[illegible table]

(b.) LOCAL REGISTRATION OF TITLE OFFICE.—Amount of Fees received in 1894, furnished by the Registrar.

[illegible table]

* Included in Central Office.

TABLE [illegible].—[illegible] made by the Registrar.

[illegible table]

TABLE [illegible].—HIGH COURT OF JUSTICE.—CONSOLIDATED TAXING OFFICE.—Return of Proceedings in the Office for the Year [illegible], made by the Masters.

[illegible table]

TABLE [illegible].—PROBATE AND MATRIMONIAL DIVISION OF THE HIGH COURT OF JUSTICE.—[illegible] RETURN of PROCEEDINGS of the DIVISION and PRINCIPAL REGISTRY in the Year [illegible].

Number of Probates [illegible] Administrations with Wills annexed	[illegible]	Number of [illegible] granted,—
" Administrations,	[illegible]	[illegible] [illegible]
" Caveats,	[illegible]	[illegible] [illegible]
" Appearances,	[illegible]	[illegible] [illegible]
" [illegible]	[illegible]	[illegible] [illegible]
" [illegible]	[illegible]	[illegible] [illegible]
" [illegible]	[illegible]	[illegible] [illegible]
" [illegible] Special Juries,	[illegible]	[illegible] [illegible]
" [illegible] Common Juries,	[illegible]	[illegible] [illegible]
" [illegible] without a Jury,	[illegible]	[illegible] [illegible]
Other [illegible]:—		[illegible] [illegible]
[illegible]	[illegible]	[illegible] [illegible]
[illegible]	[illegible]	[illegible] [illegible]
[illegible]	[illegible]	[illegible] [illegible]
[illegible]	[illegible]	
[illegible]	[illegible]	[illegible] [illegible]

TABLE [illegible].—PROBATE AND MATRIMONIAL DIVISION OF THE HIGH COURT OF JUSTICE.—MATRIMONIAL [illegible].—RETURN of PROCEEDINGS [illegible] "The [illegible] Act [illegible]" [illegible] 1[illegible], and the Matrimonial Causes and Matters, [illegible].

[illegible]	Number	[illegible]	Number
[illegible]		[illegible]	[illegible]
[illegible]	[illegible]	[illegible]	[illegible]
[illegible]	[illegible]	[illegible]	[illegible]
[illegible]	[illegible]	[illegible]	[illegible]
[illegible]	[illegible]	[illegible]	[illegible]
[illegible]	[illegible]	[illegible]	[illegible]
[illegible]	[illegible]	[illegible]	[illegible]
[illegible]	[illegible]	[illegible]	[illegible]
[illegible]	[illegible]	[illegible]	[illegible]
[illegible]	[illegible]	[illegible]	[illegible]
[illegible]	[illegible]	[illegible]	[illegible]
[illegible]	[illegible]	[illegible]	[illegible]
[illegible]	[illegible]	[illegible]	[illegible]
[illegible]	[illegible]	[illegible]	[illegible]

[illegible] Matrimonial Causes, [illegible]

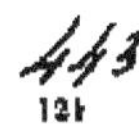

TABLE [illegible].—HIGH COURT OF JUSTICE IN IRELAND.—ADMIRALTY.—A RETURN of PROCEEDINGS in the [illegible]

NATURE OF PROCEEDINGS.	Possession.	Salvage.	Damage.	Bottomry.	[illegible]	Towage.
Instruments executed, viz.:—						
Warrants,	[illegible]	[illegible]	[illegible]		[illegible]	-
Writs of Summons,	[illegible]	-	1		-	-
Monitions for different purposes,	-	-			-	-
Attachments,	-	-	-		-	-
[illegible]	[illegible]	-	[illegible]		-	-
Decrees of Possession,	-	-	-		-	-
Releases,	[illegible]	[illegible]	[illegible]		-	-
Commissions of Appraisement,	-			-	-	-
" of Appraisement and Sale,	[illegible]		-	-	1	-
" of Delivery,			-		-	-
Total,	[illegible]	[illegible]	[illegible]	-	[illegible]	-
Arrests made of Ships,	[illegible]	-	1		[illegible]	-
" of Ships and Cargoes,	-	-	-		-	-
" of Ships and Freights,	1	-			-	-
" of Ships, Cargoes, and Freights,	[illegible]	1	-	-		-
" of Cargoes and Freights,			-	-	-	-
" of Cargoes only,	-	-	-	-	-	-
" of Freights only,	-	-	-	-	-	-
" of [illegible], &c.,	-	-	-	-	-	-
" of Proceeds in Registry,		-	-	-	-	-
Total,	[illegible]	[illegible]	[illegible]	-	[illegible]	-
Number of Bail,	[illegible]	[illegible]	[illegible]	-	-	-
Reports as to sufficiency of Bail,		-		-		-
Total,	[illegible]	[illegible]	[illegible]	-	-	-
	£ s. d.	£ s. d.	£ s. d.	£ s. d.	£ s. d.	£ s. d.
Amount of Bail required,						
Amount of Proceeds paid into Registry:—						
Of Ships sold,	777 [illegible] [illegible]	-	-		[illegible] [illegible] [illegible]	-
Of Cargoes sold,	-	-	-		-	-
Total,	777 [illegible] [illegible]	-	-	-	11 [illegible] [illegible]	-

* Court of Admiralty, Ireland.

HIGH COURT of JUSTICE in IRELAND (Admiralty) for the Year ended 31st December, 1894, made by the Registrar.

[illegible]	[illegible]	[illegible]	[illegible]	[illegible]	[illegible]	[illegible]
						Instruments [illegible]:
					[illegible]	Warrants.
			[illegible]		[illegible]	Writs of Summons.
						[illegible]
						Appearances.
			[illegible]		[illegible]	[illegible]
						[illegible]
					[illegible]	Releases.
						Commissions of appraisement.
					[illegible]	of Appraisement and Sale.
						of Delivery.
[illegible]			[illegible]		[illegible]	Total
					[illegible]	Actions [illegible] of Ships:
						[illegible]
					[illegible]	[illegible]
						of Ships, Cargoes, and Freights.
						of Cargoes and Freights.
						[illegible]
						[illegible]
						[illegible]
						[illegible]
					[illegible]	Total
					[illegible]	[illegible]
						[illegible]
[illegible]					[illegible]	Total
[illegible]	[illegible]	[illegible]	[illegible]	[illegible]	[illegible]	Amount of Bail [illegible]
						Amount of Proceeds paid into Registry:
[illegible]					[illegible]	Of Ships sold
						Of Cargoes sold
[illegible]					[illegible]	Total

[illegible]

[illegible] Cash and Securities standing to the credit of the Accountant-General of the Supreme Court of Judicature in Ireland, on 30th September, 18[illegible], viz.:—

Cash (Bank of Ireland). { Chancery Division [illegible]
{ Land Judges Division [illegible]

Securities. { Chancery Division [illegible]
{ Land Judges Division [illegible]

[illegible] during the Year to 30th September [illegible]

Chancery and Probate Law Divisions.

Dividends on Securities in Court [illegible]
Cash proceeds of sale of Securities [illegible]
Other Cash brought into Court [illegible]

Securities purchased with money in Court [illegible]
Other Securities brought into Court [illegible]

Land Judges Division.

Dividends on Securities in Court [illegible]
Cash proceeds of sale of Securities in Court [illegible]
Other Cash brought into Court [illegible]

Securities purchased with money in Court [illegible]
Other Securities brought into Court [illegible]

Chancery Division.

[illegible]

[illegible] during the Year to 30th September [illegible]

Chancery and Probate Law Divisions.

Cash paid for Securities purchased with money in Court [illegible]
Other Cash paid out of Court [illegible]

Securities sold [illegible]
Other Securities withdrawn out of Court [illegible]

Land Judges Division.

Cash paid for Securities purchased with money in Court [illegible]
Other Cash paid out of Court [illegible]

Securities sold [illegible]
Other Securities withdrawn out of Court [illegible]

Balance of Cash and Securities standing to the credit of the Accountant-General of the Supreme Court of Judicature in Ireland on 30th September, 18[illegible], viz.:—

Cash (Bank of Ireland). { Chancery Division [illegible]
{ Land Judges Division [illegible]

Securities. { Chancery Division [illegible]
{ Land Judges Division [illegible]

Chancery Division.

[illegible]

[illegible]

SUPREME COURT OF JUDICATURE, IRELAND—continued.

[illegible]

TABLE [illegible].—SUPREME COURT OF APPEAL [illegible] [illegible] 1894. [illegible]

No.	[illegible]	[illegible]	[illegible]
[illegible]	[illegible]	[illegible]	[illegible]
[illegible]	[illegible]	[illegible]	[illegible]

TABLE [illegible].—SUPREME COURT OF APPEAL.—PRIVY COUNCIL IN IRELAND.—RETURN of JUDICIAL PROCEEDINGS of the PRIVY COUNCIL in the Year 1894.

NATURE OF PROCEEDINGS.	No.	[illegible]	DISPOSED OF					Pending at [illegible]
			[illegible]					
			Granted.	Refused.	Withdrawn.	[illegible]	[illegible]	
[illegible]	[illegible]	[illegible]	[illegible]	[illegible]	[illegible]	[illegible]	[illegible]	[illegible]
[illegible]	[illegible]	[illegible]	[illegible]	[illegible]	[illegible]	[illegible]	[illegible]	[illegible]
[illegible]	[illegible]	[illegible]	[illegible]	[illegible]	[illegible]	[illegible]	[illegible]	[illegible]
[illegible]	[illegible]	[illegible]	[illegible]	[illegible]	[illegible]	[illegible]	[illegible]	[illegible]
[illegible]	[illegible]	[illegible]	[illegible]	[illegible]	[illegible]	[illegible]	[illegible]	[illegible]
[illegible]	[illegible]	[illegible]	[illegible]	[illegible]	[illegible]	[illegible]	[illegible]	[illegible]
[illegible]	[illegible]	[illegible]	[illegible]	[illegible]	[illegible]	[illegible]	[illegible]	[illegible]

[illegible]

TABLE [illegible].—SUPREME COURT OF APPEAL.—APPEALS BEFORE HER MAJESTY IN COUNCIL.—RETURN of the PROCEEDINGS of the JUDICIAL COMMITTEE of PRIVY COUNCIL in the Year 1894, made by the Registrar of the Privy Council.

Cases.	[illegible]	[illegible]	[illegible]	[illegible]
None.	None.	None.	None.	None.

TABLE [illegible].—SUPREME COURT OF APPEAL.—HOUSE OF LORDS.—RETURN of APPEALS from IRELAND in the Year 1894, made by the Clerk of the [illegible].

	Total.
[illegible]	[illegible]
[illegible]	[illegible]

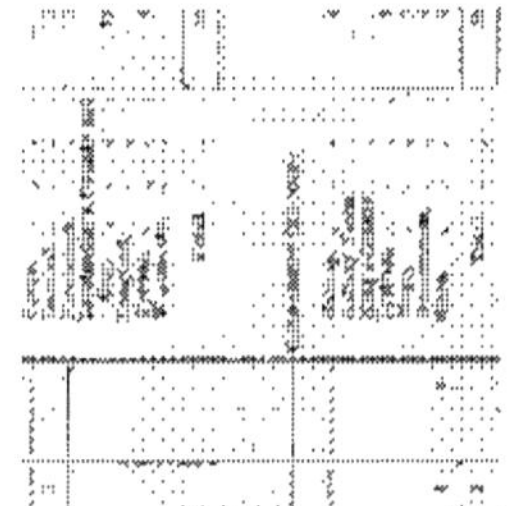

[illegible] OF THE [illegible] ENTERED FOR TRIAL

AND [illegible] IN THIS [illegible]

[illegible] Notes, Bills of Exchange, &c.
[illegible]
[illegible]
[illegible]
[illegible]

[illegible]
[illegible] for Personal Injuries and Compensation under [illegible]
[illegible]
[illegible] for Negligence.
[illegible] for Negligence.
[illegible]

[illegible]
[illegible]
[illegible]
[illegible]
[illegible]

[illegible]
[illegible] Land [illegible]
[illegible] Promise of Marriage.
[illegible]

[illegible]
[illegible]
[illegible]
[illegible]
[illegible] of [illegible]
[illegible]
[illegible] of [illegible]
[illegible]
[illegible]

TABLE [illegible].—HIGH COURT OF JUSTICE—[illegible] [illegible] JUDGES and RECORDERS in 1894, [illegible]

COUNTIES AND COUNTIES OF CITIES AND OF TOWNS [illegible] IN CIRCUITS	[illegible]	[illegible]		[illegible]
	[illegible]	[illegible]	[illegible]	
Leinster Circuit:				
Carlow,	[illegible]	[illegible]	[illegible]	[illegible]
Kildare,	[illegible]	[illegible]	[illegible]	[illegible]
Kilkenny,	[illegible]	[illegible]	[illegible]	[illegible]
Queen's County,	[illegible]	[illegible]	[illegible]	[illegible]
Tipperary, North Riding,	[illegible]	[illegible]	[illegible]	[illegible]
Tipperary, South Riding,	[illegible]	[illegible]	[illegible]	[illegible]
Waterford,	[illegible]	[illegible]	[illegible]	[illegible]
Wexford,	[illegible]	[illegible]	[illegible]	[illegible]
Wicklow,	[illegible]	[illegible]	[illegible]	[illegible]
Total,	[illegible]	[illegible]	[illegible]	[illegible]
Munster Circuit:				
Clare,	[illegible]	[illegible]	[illegible]	[illegible]
Cork, East Riding,	[illegible]	[illegible]	[illegible]	[illegible]
Cork, West Riding,	[illegible]	[illegible]	[illegible]	[illegible]
Kerry,	[illegible]	[illegible]	[illegible]	[illegible]
Limerick,	[illegible]	[illegible]	[illegible]	[illegible]
Total,	[illegible]	[illegible]	[illegible]	[illegible]
North-East Circuit:				
Antrim,	[illegible]	[illegible]	[illegible]	[illegible]
Armagh,	[illegible]	[illegible]	[illegible]	[illegible]
Down,	[illegible]	[illegible]	[illegible]	[illegible]
Louth,	[illegible]	[illegible]	[illegible]	[illegible]
Meath,	[illegible]	[illegible]	[illegible]	[illegible]
Monaghan,	[illegible]	[illegible]	[illegible]	[illegible]
Total,	[illegible]	[illegible]	[illegible]	[illegible]
North-West Circuit:				
Cavan,	[illegible]	[illegible]	[illegible]	[illegible]
Donegal,	[illegible]	[illegible]	[illegible]	[illegible]
Fermanagh,	[illegible]	[illegible]	[illegible]	[illegible]
Londonderry,	[illegible]	[illegible]	[illegible]	[illegible]
Longford,	[illegible]	[illegible]	[illegible]	[illegible]
Tyrone,	[illegible]	[illegible]	[illegible]	[illegible]
Westmeath,	[illegible]	[illegible]	[illegible]	[illegible]
Total,	[illegible]	[illegible]	[illegible]	[illegible]
Connaught Circuit:				
Galway,	[illegible]	[illegible]	[illegible]	[illegible]
King's County,	[illegible]	[illegible]	[illegible]	[illegible]
Leitrim,	[illegible]	[illegible]	[illegible]	[illegible]
Mayo,	[illegible]	[illegible]	[illegible]	[illegible]
Roscommon,	[illegible]	[illegible]	[illegible]	[illegible]
Sligo,	[illegible]	[illegible]	[illegible]	[illegible]
Total,	[illegible]	[illegible]	[illegible]	[illegible]
Belfast City, [illegible]	[illegible]	[illegible]	[illegible]	[illegible]
Cork City, [illegible]	[illegible]	[illegible]	[illegible]	[illegible]
[illegible] Town, [illegible]	[illegible]	[illegible]	[illegible]	[illegible]
Londonderry City, [illegible]	[illegible]	[illegible]	[illegible]	[illegible]
Total,	[illegible]	[illegible]	[illegible]	[illegible]
Total of Ireland,	[illegible]	[illegible]	[illegible]	[illegible]

TABLE [illegible].—COUNTY COURTS AND RECORDERS' COURTS.—CIVIL BILL EJECTMENTS, REPLEVINS, and other CIVIL BILLS served by CIVIL BILL OFFICERS in [illegible] [illegible] made by Civil Bill Officers appointed by COUNTY COURT JUDGES and RECORDERS.

[illegible]	[illegible]	[illegible]	[illegible]	[illegible]		
				Civil Bill Ejectments	Replevins	Other Civil Bills
Leinster.						
Carlow,	[illegible]	[illegible]	..	[illegible]	[illegible]	[illegible]
Dublin,	[illegible]	[illegible]	[illegible]	[illegible]	[illegible]	[illegible]
Dublin City,	[illegible]	[illegible]	[illegible]	[illegible]	[illegible]	[illegible]
Kildare,	[illegible]	[illegible]	[illegible]	[illegible]	[illegible]	[illegible]
Kilkenny and City,	[illegible]	[illegible]	..	[illegible]	[illegible]	[illegible]
King's County,	[illegible]	[illegible]	[illegible]	[illegible]	[illegible]	[illegible]
Longford,	[illegible]	[illegible]	[illegible]	[illegible]	[illegible]	[illegible]
Louth and Drogheda Town,	[illegible]	[illegible]	[illegible]	[illegible]	[illegible]	[illegible]
Meath,	[illegible]	[illegible]	[illegible]	[illegible]	[illegible]	[illegible]
Queen's County,	[illegible]	[illegible]	[illegible]	[illegible]	[illegible]	[illegible]
Westmeath,	[illegible]	[illegible]	[illegible]	[illegible]	[illegible]	[illegible]
Wexford,	[illegible]	[illegible]	[illegible]	[illegible]	[illegible]	[illegible]
Wicklow,	[illegible]	[illegible]	[illegible]	[illegible]	[illegible]	[illegible]

[illegible]

COUNTIES.	[illegible]	[illegible]	[illegible]	[illegible]	[illegible]	[illegible]	[illegible]	[illegible]	[illegible]	[illegible]	[illegible]	[illegible]	[illegible]
LEINSTER:													
Carlow,	[illegible]	[illegible]	[illegible]	[illegible]	[illegible]	[illegible]	[illegible]	[illegible]	[illegible]	[illegible]	[illegible]	[illegible]	[illegible]
Dublin,	[illegible]	[illegible]	[illegible]	[illegible]	[illegible]	[illegible]	[illegible]	[illegible]	[illegible]	[illegible]	[illegible]	[illegible]	[illegible]
Dublin City,	[illegible]	[illegible]	[illegible]	[illegible]	[illegible]	[illegible]	[illegible]	[illegible]	[illegible]	[illegible]	[illegible]	[illegible]	[illegible]
Kildare,	[illegible]	[illegible]	[illegible]	[illegible]	[illegible]	[illegible]	[illegible]	[illegible]	[illegible]	[illegible]	[illegible]	[illegible]	[illegible]
Kilkenny,	[illegible]	[illegible]	[illegible]	[illegible]	[illegible]	[illegible]	[illegible]	[illegible]	[illegible]	[illegible]	[illegible]	[illegible]	[illegible]
King's County,	[illegible]	[illegible]	[illegible]	[illegible]	[illegible]	[illegible]	[illegible]	[illegible]	[illegible]	[illegible]	[illegible]	[illegible]	[illegible]
Longford,	[illegible]	[illegible]	[illegible]	[illegible]	[illegible]	[illegible]	[illegible]	[illegible]	[illegible]	[illegible]	[illegible]	[illegible]	[illegible]
Louth,	[illegible]	[illegible]	[illegible]	[illegible]	[illegible]	[illegible]	[illegible]	[illegible]	[illegible]	[illegible]	[illegible]	[illegible]	[illegible]
Meath,	[illegible]	[illegible]	[illegible]	[illegible]	[illegible]	[illegible]	[illegible]	[illegible]	[illegible]	[illegible]	[illegible]	[illegible]	[illegible]
Queen's County,	[illegible]	[illegible]	[illegible]	[illegible]	[illegible]	[illegible]	[illegible]	[illegible]	[illegible]	[illegible]	[illegible]	[illegible]	[illegible]
Westmeath,	[illegible]	[illegible]	[illegible]	[illegible]	[illegible]	[illegible]	[illegible]	[illegible]	[illegible]	[illegible]	[illegible]	[illegible]	[illegible]
Wexford,	[illegible]	[illegible]	[illegible]	[illegible]	[illegible]	[illegible]	[illegible]	[illegible]	[illegible]	[illegible]	[illegible]	[illegible]	[illegible]
Wicklow,	[illegible]	[illegible]	[illegible]	[illegible]	[illegible]	[illegible]	[illegible]	[illegible]	[illegible]	[illegible]	[illegible]	[illegible]	[illegible]
Total,	[illegible]	[illegible]	[illegible]	[illegible]	[illegible]	[illegible]	[illegible]	[illegible]	[illegible]	[illegible]	[illegible]	[illegible]	[illegible]
MUNSTER:													
Clare,	[illegible]	[illegible]	[illegible]	[illegible]	[illegible]	[illegible]	[illegible]	[illegible]	[illegible]	[illegible]	[illegible]	[illegible]	[illegible]
Cork, East Riding,	[illegible]	[illegible]	[illegible]	[illegible]	[illegible]	[illegible]	[illegible]	[illegible]	[illegible]	[illegible]	[illegible]	[illegible]	[illegible]
Cork, West Riding,	[illegible]	[illegible]	[illegible]	[illegible]	[illegible]	[illegible]	[illegible]	[illegible]	[illegible]	[illegible]	[illegible]	[illegible]	[illegible]
Kerry,	[illegible]	[illegible]	[illegible]	[illegible]	[illegible]	[illegible]	[illegible]	[illegible]	[illegible]	[illegible]	[illegible]	[illegible]	[illegible]
Limerick,	[illegible]	[illegible]	[illegible]	[illegible]	[illegible]	[illegible]	[illegible]	[illegible]	[illegible]	[illegible]	[illegible]	[illegible]	[illegible]
Tipperary,	[illegible]	[illegible]	[illegible]	[illegible]	[illegible]	[illegible]	[illegible]	[illegible]	[illegible]	[illegible]	[illegible]	[illegible]	[illegible]
Waterford,	[illegible]	[illegible]	[illegible]	[illegible]	[illegible]	[illegible]	[illegible]	[illegible]	[illegible]	[illegible]	[illegible]	[illegible]	[illegible]
Total,	[illegible]	[illegible]	[illegible]	[illegible]	[illegible]	[illegible]	[illegible]	[illegible]	[illegible]	[illegible]	[illegible]	[illegible]	[illegible]
ULSTER:													
Antrim,	[illegible]	[illegible]	[illegible]	[illegible]	[illegible]	[illegible]	[illegible]	[illegible]	[illegible]	[illegible]	[illegible]	[illegible]	[illegible]
Armagh,	[illegible]	[illegible]	[illegible]	[illegible]	[illegible]	[illegible]	[illegible]	[illegible]	[illegible]	[illegible]	[illegible]	[illegible]	[illegible]
Cavan,	[illegible]	[illegible]	[illegible]	[illegible]	[illegible]	[illegible]	[illegible]	[illegible]	[illegible]	[illegible]	[illegible]	[illegible]	[illegible]
Donegal,	[illegible]	[illegible]	[illegible]	[illegible]	[illegible]	[illegible]	[illegible]	[illegible]	[illegible]	[illegible]	[illegible]	[illegible]	[illegible]
Down,	[illegible]	[illegible]	[illegible]	[illegible]	[illegible]	[illegible]	[illegible]	[illegible]	[illegible]	[illegible]	[illegible]	[illegible]	[illegible]
Fermanagh,	[illegible]	[illegible]	[illegible]	[illegible]	[illegible]	[illegible]	[illegible]	[illegible]	[illegible]	[illegible]	[illegible]	[illegible]	[illegible]
Londonderry,	[illegible]	[illegible]	[illegible]	[illegible]	[illegible]	[illegible]	[illegible]	[illegible]	[illegible]	[illegible]	[illegible]	[illegible]	[illegible]
Monaghan,	[illegible]	[illegible]	[illegible]	[illegible]	[illegible]	[illegible]	[illegible]	[illegible]	[illegible]	[illegible]	[illegible]	[illegible]	[illegible]
Tyrone,	[illegible]	[illegible]	[illegible]	[illegible]	[illegible]	[illegible]	[illegible]	[illegible]	[illegible]	[illegible]	[illegible]	[illegible]	[illegible]
Total,	[illegible]	[illegible]	[illegible]	[illegible]	[illegible]	[illegible]	[illegible]	[illegible]	[illegible]	[illegible]	[illegible]	[illegible]	[illegible]
CONNAUGHT:													
Galway,	[illegible]	[illegible]	[illegible]	[illegible]	[illegible]	[illegible]	[illegible]	[illegible]	[illegible]	[illegible]	[illegible]	[illegible]	[illegible]
Leitrim,	[illegible]	[illegible]	[illegible]	[illegible]	[illegible]	[illegible]	[illegible]	[illegible]	[illegible]	[illegible]	[illegible]	[illegible]	[illegible]
Mayo,	[illegible]	[illegible]	[illegible]	[illegible]	[illegible]	[illegible]	[illegible]	[illegible]	[illegible]	[illegible]	[illegible]	[illegible]	[illegible]
Roscommon,	[illegible]	[illegible]	[illegible]	[illegible]	[illegible]	[illegible]	[illegible]	[illegible]	[illegible]	[illegible]	[illegible]	[illegible]	[illegible]
Sligo,	[illegible]	[illegible]	[illegible]	[illegible]	[illegible]	[illegible]	[illegible]	[illegible]	[illegible]	[illegible]	[illegible]	[illegible]	[illegible]
Total,	[illegible]	[illegible]	[illegible]	[illegible]	[illegible]	[illegible]	[illegible]	[illegible]	[illegible]	[illegible]	[illegible]	[illegible]	[illegible]
Total of Ireland,	[illegible]	[illegible]	[illegible]	[illegible]	[illegible]	[illegible]	[illegible]	[illegible]	[illegible]	[illegible]	[illegible]	[illegible]	[illegible]

	[illegible]	[illegible]						Leinster.
[illegible]	[illegible]	[illegible]	[illegible]					Carlow.
	[illegible]	[illegible]	[illegible]	[illegible]				Dublin.
[illegible]	[illegible]	[illegible]	[illegible]			[illegible]		Dublin City.
	[illegible]	[illegible]	[illegible]		[illegible]	[illegible]		Kildare.
	[illegible]	[illegible]	[illegible]	[illegible]		[illegible]		Kilkenny.
	[illegible]	[illegible]	[illegible]	[illegible]				King's County.
	[illegible]	[illegible]	[illegible]					Longford.
[illegible]	[illegible]	[illegible]	[illegible]	[illegible]				Louth.
[illegible]	[illegible]	[illegible]	[illegible]	[illegible]				Meath.
	[illegible]	[illegible]	[illegible]			[illegible]		Queen's County.
	[illegible]		[illegible]					Westmeath.
	[illegible]	[illegible]	[illegible]					Wexford.
		[illegible]	[illegible]					Wicklow.
	[illegible]	[illegible]	[illegible]	[illegible]		[illegible]		Total.
								Munster.
[illegible]	[illegible]	[illegible]	[illegible]	[illegible]	[illegible]	[illegible]		Clare.
[illegible]	[illegible]	[illegible]	[illegible]	[illegible]				Cork, East Riding.
	[illegible]	[illegible]	[illegible]	[illegible]		[illegible]		Cork, West Riding.
	[illegible]	[illegible]	[illegible]	[illegible]		[illegible]		Kerry.
	[illegible]	[illegible]	[illegible]	[illegible]		[illegible]		Limerick.
	[illegible]	[illegible]	[illegible]	[illegible]		[illegible]		Tipperary.
[illegible]	[illegible]	[illegible]	[illegible]	[illegible]	[illegible]	[illegible]		Waterford.
[illegible]	[illegible]	[illegible]	[illegible]	[illegible]	[illegible]	[illegible]		Total.
								Ulster.
[illegible]	[illegible]		[illegible]	[illegible]				Antrim.
	[illegible]	[illegible]	[illegible]			[illegible]		Armagh.
[illegible]	[illegible]		[illegible]	[illegible]				Cavan.
	[illegible]	[illegible]	[illegible]	[illegible]				Donegal.
[illegible]	[illegible]	[illegible]	[illegible]	[illegible]				Down.
[illegible]	[illegible]	[illegible]	[illegible]			[illegible]		Fermanagh.
	[illegible]	[illegible]	[illegible]	[illegible]				Londonderry.
	[illegible]	[illegible]	[illegible]	[illegible]		[illegible]		Monaghan.
	[illegible]	[illegible]	[illegible]	[illegible]				Tyrone.
[illegible]	[illegible]	[illegible]	[illegible]	[illegible]		[illegible]		Total.
								Connaught.
		[illegible]	[illegible]	[illegible]				Galway.
	[illegible]	[illegible]						Leitrim.
	[illegible]	[illegible]	[illegible]	[illegible]				Mayo.
			[illegible]	[illegible]				Roscommon.
	[illegible]	[illegible]	[illegible]	[illegible]				Sligo.
	[illegible]	[illegible]	[illegible]	[illegible]				Total.
[illegible]	[illegible]	[illegible]	[illegible]	[illegible]	[illegible]	[illegible]		Total of Ireland.

[illegible]

Leinster:	[illegible]
Carlow.	[illegible]
Dublin.	[illegible]
Kildare.	[illegible]
Kilkenny.	[illegible]
King's County.	[illegible]
Longford.	[illegible]
Louth.	[illegible]
Meath.	[illegible]
Queen's County.	[illegible]
Westmeath.	[illegible]
Wexford.	[illegible]
Wicklow.	[illegible]
Total of Leinster.	[illegible]
Munster:	
Clare.	[illegible]
Cork, E.R.	[illegible]
Cork, W.R.	[illegible]
Kerry.	[illegible]
Limerick.	[illegible]
Tipperary.	[illegible]
Waterford.	[illegible]
Total of Munster.	[illegible]
Ulster:	
Antrim.	[illegible]
Armagh.	[illegible]
Cavan.	[illegible]
Donegal.	[illegible]
Down.	[illegible]
Fermanagh.	[illegible]
Londonderry.	[illegible]
Monaghan.	[illegible]
Tyrone.	[illegible]
Total of Ulster.	[illegible]
Connaught:	
Galway.	[illegible]
Leitrim.	[illegible]
Mayo.	[illegible]
Roscommon.	[illegible]
Sligo.	[illegible]
Total of Connaught.	[illegible]
Total of Ireland.	[illegible]

Provinces, Counties, and Boroughs.	[illegible]	[illegible]	[illegible]	[illegible]	[illegible]	[illegible]	[illegible]	[illegible]	[illegible]	[illegible]
Leinster:	£.	£.	£.	£.	£.	£.	£.	£.	£.	£.
Carlow,	[illegible]	[illegible]	[illegible]	[illegible]	[illegible]	[illegible]	[illegible]	[illegible]	[illegible]	[illegible]
Dublin,	[illegible]	[illegible]	[illegible]	[illegible]	[illegible]	[illegible]	[illegible]	[illegible]	[illegible]	[illegible]
Kildare,	[illegible]	[illegible]	[illegible]	[illegible]	[illegible]	[illegible]	[illegible]	[illegible]	[illegible]	[illegible]
Kilkenny,	[illegible]	[illegible]	[illegible]	[illegible]	[illegible]	[illegible]	[illegible]	[illegible]	[illegible]	[illegible]
King's County,	[illegible]	[illegible]	[illegible]	[illegible]	[illegible]	[illegible]	[illegible]	[illegible]	[illegible]	[illegible]
Longford,	[illegible]	[illegible]	[illegible]	[illegible]	[illegible]	[illegible]	[illegible]	[illegible]	[illegible]	[illegible]
Louth,	[illegible]	[illegible]	[illegible]	[illegible]	[illegible]	[illegible]	[illegible]	[illegible]	[illegible]	[illegible]
Meath,	[illegible]	[illegible]	[illegible]	[illegible]	[illegible]	[illegible]	[illegible]	[illegible]	[illegible]	[illegible]
Queen's County,	[illegible]	[illegible]	[illegible]	[illegible]	[illegible]	[illegible]	[illegible]	[illegible]	[illegible]	[illegible]
Westmeath,	[illegible]	[illegible]	[illegible]	[illegible]	[illegible]	[illegible]	[illegible]	[illegible]	[illegible]	[illegible]
Wexford,	[illegible]	[illegible]	[illegible]	[illegible]	[illegible]	[illegible]	[illegible]	[illegible]	[illegible]	[illegible]
Wicklow,	[illegible]	[illegible]	[illegible]	[illegible]	[illegible]	[illegible]	[illegible]	[illegible]	[illegible]	[illegible]
Total of Leinster,	[illegible]	[illegible]	[illegible]	[illegible]	[illegible]	[illegible]	[illegible]	[illegible]	[illegible]	[illegible]
Munster:										
Clare,	[illegible]	[illegible]	[illegible]	[illegible]	[illegible]	[illegible]	[illegible]	[illegible]	[illegible]	[illegible]
Cork, E.R.,	[illegible]	[illegible]	[illegible]	[illegible]	[illegible]	[illegible]	[illegible]	[illegible]	[illegible]	[illegible]
Cork, W.R.,	[illegible]	[illegible]	[illegible]	[illegible]	[illegible]	[illegible]	[illegible]	[illegible]	[illegible]	[illegible]
Kerry,	[illegible]	[illegible]	[illegible]	[illegible]	[illegible]	[illegible]	[illegible]	[illegible]	[illegible]	[illegible]
Limerick,	[illegible]	[illegible]	[illegible]	[illegible]	[illegible]	[illegible]	[illegible]	[illegible]	[illegible]	[illegible]
Tipperary,	[illegible]	[illegible]	[illegible]	[illegible]	[illegible]	[illegible]	[illegible]	[illegible]	[illegible]	[illegible]
Waterford,	[illegible]	[illegible]	[illegible]	[illegible]	[illegible]	[illegible]	[illegible]	[illegible]	[illegible]	[illegible]
Total of Munster,	[illegible]	[illegible]	[illegible]	[illegible]	[illegible]	[illegible]	[illegible]	[illegible]	[illegible]	[illegible]
Ulster:										
Antrim,	[illegible]	[illegible]	[illegible]	[illegible]	[illegible]	[illegible]	[illegible]	[illegible]	[illegible]	[illegible]
Armagh,	[illegible]	[illegible]	[illegible]	[illegible]	[illegible]	[illegible]	[illegible]	[illegible]	[illegible]	[illegible]
Cavan,	[illegible]	[illegible]	[illegible]	[illegible]	[illegible]	[illegible]	[illegible]	[illegible]	[illegible]	[illegible]
Donegal,	[illegible]	[illegible]	[illegible]	[illegible]	[illegible]	[illegible]	[illegible]	[illegible]	[illegible]	[illegible]
Down,	[illegible]	[illegible]	[illegible]	[illegible]	[illegible]	[illegible]	[illegible]	[illegible]	[illegible]	[illegible]
Fermanagh,	[illegible]	[illegible]	[illegible]	[illegible]	[illegible]	[illegible]	[illegible]	[illegible]	[illegible]	[illegible]
Londonderry,	[illegible]	[illegible]	[illegible]	[illegible]	[illegible]	[illegible]	[illegible]	[illegible]	[illegible]	[illegible]
Monaghan,	[illegible]	[illegible]	[illegible]	[illegible]	[illegible]	[illegible]	[illegible]	[illegible]	[illegible]	[illegible]
Tyrone,	[illegible]	[illegible]	[illegible]	[illegible]	[illegible]	[illegible]	[illegible]	[illegible]	[illegible]	[illegible]
Total of Ulster,	[illegible]	[illegible]	[illegible]	[illegible]	[illegible]	[illegible]	[illegible]	[illegible]	[illegible]	[illegible]
Connaught:										
Galway,	[illegible]	[illegible]	[illegible]	[illegible]	[illegible]	[illegible]	[illegible]	[illegible]	[illegible]	[illegible]
Leitrim,	[illegible]	[illegible]	[illegible]	[illegible]	[illegible]	[illegible]	[illegible]	[illegible]	[illegible]	[illegible]
Mayo,	[illegible]	[illegible]	[illegible]	[illegible]	[illegible]	[illegible]	[illegible]	[illegible]	[illegible]	[illegible]
Roscommon,	[illegible]	[illegible]	[illegible]	[illegible]	[illegible]	[illegible]	[illegible]	[illegible]	[illegible]	[illegible]
Sligo,	[illegible]	[illegible]	[illegible]	[illegible]	[illegible]	[illegible]	[illegible]	[illegible]	[illegible]	[illegible]
Total of Connaught,	[illegible]	[illegible]	[illegible]	[illegible]	[illegible]	[illegible]	[illegible]	[illegible]	[illegible]	[illegible]
Total of Ireland,	[illegible]	[illegible]	[illegible]	[illegible]	[illegible]	[illegible]	[illegible]	[illegible]	[illegible]	[illegible]

[illegible]	[illegible]
Leinster	[illegible]
Carlow	[illegible]
Dublin	[illegible]
Kildare	[illegible]
Kilkenny	[illegible]
King's County	[illegible]
Longford	[illegible]
Louth	[illegible]
Meath	[illegible]
Queen's County	[illegible]
Westmeath	[illegible]
Wexford	[illegible]
Wicklow	[illegible]
Total of Leinster	[illegible]
Munster	
Clare	[illegible]
Cork, E.R.	[illegible]
Cork, W.R.	[illegible]
Kerry	[illegible]
Limerick	[illegible]
Tipperary	[illegible]
Waterford	[illegible]
Total of Munster	[illegible]
Ulster	
Antrim	[illegible]
Armagh	[illegible]
Cavan	[illegible]
Donegal	[illegible]
Down	[illegible]
Fermanagh	[illegible]
Londonderry	[illegible]
Monaghan	[illegible]
Tyrone	[illegible]
Total of Ulster	[illegible]
Connaught	
Galway	[illegible]
Leitrim	[illegible]
Mayo	[illegible]
Roscommon	[illegible]
Sligo	[illegible]
Total of Connaught	[illegible]

Counties arranged in Provinces.	[illegible]				
	[illegible]	[illegible]	[illegible]	[illegible]	[illegible]
Leinster.					
Carlow,	[illegible]	[illegible]	[illegible]	[illegible]	[illegible]
Dublin,	[illegible]	[illegible]	[illegible]	[illegible]	[illegible]
Kildare,	[illegible]	[illegible]	[illegible]	[illegible]	[illegible]
Kilkenny,	[illegible]	[illegible]	[illegible]	[illegible]	[illegible]
King's County,	[illegible]	[illegible]	[illegible]	[illegible]	[illegible]
Longford,	[illegible]	[illegible]	[illegible]	[illegible]	[illegible]
Louth,	[illegible]	[illegible]	[illegible]	[illegible]	[illegible]
Meath,	[illegible]	[illegible]	[illegible]	[illegible]	[illegible]
Queen's County,	[illegible]	[illegible]	[illegible]	[illegible]	[illegible]
Westmeath,	[illegible]	[illegible]	[illegible]	[illegible]	[illegible]
Wexford,	[illegible]	[illegible]	[illegible]	[illegible]	[illegible]
Wicklow,	[illegible]	[illegible]	[illegible]	[illegible]	[illegible]
Total of Leinster,	[illegible]	[illegible]	[illegible]	[illegible]	[illegible]
Munster.					
Clare,	[illegible]	[illegible]	[illegible]	[illegible]	[illegible]
Cork,	[illegible]	[illegible]	[illegible]	[illegible]	[illegible]
Kerry,	[illegible]	[illegible]	[illegible]	[illegible]	[illegible]
Limerick,	[illegible]	[illegible]	[illegible]	[illegible]	[illegible]
Tipperary,	[illegible]	[illegible]	[illegible]	[illegible]	[illegible]
Waterford,	[illegible]	[illegible]	[illegible]	[illegible]	[illegible]
Total of Munster,	[illegible]	[illegible]	[illegible]	[illegible]	[illegible]
Ulster.					
Antrim,	[illegible]	[illegible]	[illegible]	[illegible]	[illegible]
Armagh,	[illegible]	[illegible]	[illegible]	[illegible]	[illegible]
Cavan,	[illegible]	[illegible]	[illegible]	[illegible]	[illegible]
Donegal,	[illegible]	[illegible]	[illegible]	[illegible]	[illegible]
Down,	[illegible]	[illegible]	[illegible]	[illegible]	[illegible]
Fermanagh,	[illegible]	[illegible]	[illegible]	[illegible]	[illegible]
Londonderry,	[illegible]	[illegible]	[illegible]	[illegible]	[illegible]
Monaghan,	[illegible]	[illegible]	[illegible]	[illegible]	[illegible]
Tyrone,	[illegible]	[illegible]	[illegible]	[illegible]	[illegible]
Total of Ulster,	[illegible]	[illegible]	[illegible]	[illegible]	[illegible]

[illegible]		[illegible]				[illegible]
[illegible]	[illegible]	[illegible]	[illegible]	[illegible]	[illegible]	
[illegible]	[illegible]	[illegible]	[illegible]	[illegible]	[illegible]	Carlow
[illegible]	[illegible]	[illegible]	[illegible]	[illegible]	[illegible]	Dublin
[illegible]	[illegible]	[illegible]	[illegible]	[illegible]	[illegible]	Kildare
[illegible]	[illegible]	[illegible]	[illegible]	[illegible]	[illegible]	Kilkenny
[illegible]	[illegible]	[illegible]	[illegible]	[illegible]	[illegible]	King's County
[illegible]	[illegible]	[illegible]	[illegible]	[illegible]	[illegible]	Longford
[illegible]	[illegible]	[illegible]	[illegible]	[illegible]	[illegible]	Louth
[illegible]	[illegible]	[illegible]	[illegible]	[illegible]	[illegible]	Meath
[illegible]	[illegible]	[illegible]	[illegible]	[illegible]	[illegible]	Queen's County
[illegible]	[illegible]	[illegible]	[illegible]	[illegible]	[illegible]	Westmeath
[illegible]	[illegible]	[illegible]	[illegible]	[illegible]	[illegible]	Wexford
[illegible]	[illegible]	[illegible]	[illegible]	[illegible]	[illegible]	Wicklow
[illegible]	[illegible]	[illegible]	[illegible]	[illegible]	[illegible]	Total of Leinster
						Munster:
[illegible]	[illegible]	[illegible]	[illegible]	[illegible]	[illegible]	Clare
[illegible]	[illegible]	[illegible]	[illegible]	[illegible]	[illegible]	Cork
[illegible]	[illegible]	[illegible]	[illegible]	[illegible]	[illegible]	Kerry
[illegible]	[illegible]	[illegible]	[illegible]	[illegible]	[illegible]	Limerick
[illegible]	[illegible]	[illegible]	[illegible]	[illegible]	[illegible]	Tipperary
[illegible]	[illegible]	[illegible]	[illegible]	[illegible]	[illegible]	Waterford
[illegible]	[illegible]	[illegible]	[illegible]	[illegible]	[illegible]	Total of Munster
						Ulster:
[illegible]	[illegible]	[illegible]	[illegible]	[illegible]	[illegible]	Antrim
[illegible]	[illegible]	[illegible]	[illegible]	[illegible]	[illegible]	Armagh
[illegible]	[illegible]	[illegible]	[illegible]	[illegible]	[illegible]	Cavan
[illegible]	[illegible]	[illegible]	[illegible]	[illegible]	[illegible]	Donegal
[illegible]	[illegible]	[illegible]	[illegible]	[illegible]	[illegible]	Down
[illegible]	[illegible]	[illegible]	[illegible]	[illegible]	[illegible]	Fermanagh
[illegible]	[illegible]	[illegible]	[illegible]	[illegible]	[illegible]	Londonderry
[illegible]	[illegible]	[illegible]	[illegible]	[illegible]	[illegible]	Monaghan
[illegible]	[illegible]	[illegible]	[illegible]	[illegible]	[illegible]	Tyrone
[illegible]	[illegible]	[illegible]	[illegible]	[illegible]	[illegible]	Total of Ulster
						Connaught:
[illegible]	[illegible]	[illegible]	[illegible]	[illegible]	[illegible]	Galway
[illegible]	[illegible]	[illegible]	[illegible]	[illegible]	[illegible]	Leitrim
[illegible]	[illegible]	[illegible]	[illegible]	[illegible]	[illegible]	Mayo
[illegible]	[illegible]	[illegible]	[illegible]	[illegible]	[illegible]	Roscommon

[illegible]											
Writs of Execution from High Court of Justice.											
[illegible]	[illegible]	[illegible]	[illegible]	[illegible]	[illegible]	[illegible]	[illegible]	[illegible]	[illegible]	[illegible]	[illegible]
[illegible]	[illegible]	[illegible]		[illegible]		[illegible]					
[illegible]											
Total Number of [illegible]	[illegible]	[illegible]	[illegible]	[illegible]	[illegible]	220	[illegible]	[illegible]	[illegible]	[illegible]	
[illegible]	[illegible]	[illegible]			[illegible]	[illegible]	[illegible]	[illegible]	[illegible]	[illegible]	
[illegible]	[illegible]										
[illegible]	[illegible]	[illegible]	[illegible]	[illegible]	[illegible]	[illegible]	[illegible]	[illegible]	[illegible]	[illegible]	
Total Number of [illegible]	[illegible]	[illegible]			[illegible]	[illegible]		[illegible]			
[illegible]	[illegible]	[illegible]			[illegible]	[illegible]		[illegible]			
[illegible]	[illegible]										
[illegible]	[illegible]	[illegible]			[illegible]	[illegible]					
Total Number of [illegible]	408	[illegible]	[illegible]					[illegible]	[illegible]		
[illegible]	[illegible]	[illegible]	[illegible]					[illegible]	[illegible]		
[illegible]	[illegible]										
[illegible]	[illegible]	[illegible]	[illegible]								
Total Number of [illegible]	[illegible]	[illegible]	[illegible]	[illegible]	[illegible]	[illegible]	[illegible]	[illegible]	[illegible]	[illegible]	[illegible]
[illegible]	[illegible]	[illegible]	[illegible]	[illegible]							
[illegible]	[illegible]	[illegible]	[illegible]	[illegible]							
[illegible]											

IRELAND.

[illegible] to Quarter Sessions									
(1) [illegible]									
(2) [illegible]									
(3) [illegible]									
[illegible] Proceedings [illegible]									
[illegible]									
[illegible] Writs of [illegible]	[illegible]				[illegible]	[illegible]			[illegible]
[illegible]	[illegible]	[illegible]							[illegible]
[illegible]	[illegible]	[illegible]							[illegible]
[illegible] Affidavits [illegible]									
[illegible] High Court [illegible]									
Final Process	[illegible]	[illegible]	[illegible]	[illegible]	[illegible]	[illegible]	[illegible]	[illegible]	[illegible]
[illegible]	[illegible]	[illegible]						[illegible]	
[illegible]									
Number of Judgments [illegible]	[illegible]	[illegible]	[illegible]		[illegible]	[illegible]	[illegible]	[illegible]	[illegible]
[illegible] High Court [illegible]	[illegible]	[illegible]	[illegible]					[illegible]	[illegible]
by Special Judge	[illegible]		[illegible]	[illegible]				[illegible]	
Total [illegible]	[illegible]	[illegible]	[illegible]		[illegible]	[illegible]	[illegible]		[illegible]
Number of Judgments [illegible]	[illegible]	[illegible]	[illegible]		[illegible]	[illegible]	[illegible]	[illegible]	[illegible]
[illegible] High Court of Justice [illegible]	[illegible]	[illegible]		[illegible]	[illegible]		[illegible]		[illegible]
by Special Judge	[illegible]		[illegible]						[illegible]
Total [illegible]	[illegible]	[illegible]	[illegible]		[illegible]	[illegible]	[illegible]	[illegible]	
Number of Judgments [illegible]	[illegible]	[illegible]	[illegible]		[illegible]	[illegible]			[illegible]
[illegible]	[illegible]	[illegible]			[illegible]				
by Special Judge									
Total [illegible]	[illegible]	[illegible]	[illegible]		[illegible]	[illegible]			[illegible]
Number of [illegible]	[illegible]	[illegible]	[illegible]		[illegible]	[illegible]	[illegible]	[illegible]	[illegible]
[illegible]	[illegible]	[illegible]							
[illegible]	[illegible]	[illegible]							
[illegible]									
[illegible]									
[illegible]									
[illegible]									
[illegible]									
[illegible]									
[illegible]	[illegible]	[illegible]			[illegible]	[illegible]			

[illegible]	[illegible]
[illegible]	[illegible]
[illegible]	[illegible]
[illegible]	[illegible]
[illegible]	42
[illegible]	[illegible]
[illegible]	[illegible]
[illegible]	[illegible]

[illegible]							
[illegible]	[illegible]	[illegible]	[illegible]	[illegible]	[illegible]	[illegible]	[illegible]
Total of [illegible]	[illegible]	[illegible]	[illegible]	[illegible]	[illegible]	[illegible]	[illegible]
[illegible]	[illegible]	[illegible]	[illegible]	[illegible]	[illegible]	[illegible]	[illegible]
Total of [illegible]	[illegible]	[illegible]	[illegible]	[illegible]	[illegible]	[illegible]	[illegible]
[illegible]	[illegible]	[illegible]	[illegible]	[illegible]	[illegible]	[illegible]	[illegible]
Total of [illegible]	[illegible]	[illegible]	[illegible]	[illegible]	[illegible]	[illegible]	[illegible]
[illegible]	[illegible]	[illegible]	[illegible]	[illegible]	[illegible]	[illegible]	[illegible]
Total of [illegible]	[illegible]	[illegible]	[illegible]	[illegible]	[illegible]	[illegible]	[illegible]
[illegible]	[illegible]	[illegible]	[illegible]	[illegible]	[illegible]	[illegible]	[illegible]

[illegible]

[illegible]	[illegible]				[illegible]			
	[illegible]	[illegible]	[illegible]	[illegible]	[illegible]	[illegible]	[illegible]	[illegible]
[illegible]	[illegible]	[illegible]	[illegible]	[illegible]	[illegible]	[illegible]	[illegible]	[illegible]
[illegible]	[illegible]				[illegible]	[illegible]	[illegible]	[illegible]
[illegible]	[illegible]	[illegible]	[illegible]	[illegible]	[illegible]	[illegible]	[illegible]	[illegible]
[illegible]	[illegible]	[illegible]	[illegible]	[illegible]	[illegible]	[illegible]	[illegible]	[illegible]
[illegible]	[illegible]	[illegible]	[illegible]	[illegible]	[illegible]	[illegible]	[illegible]	[illegible]
[illegible]	[illegible]	[illegible]	[illegible]	[illegible]	[illegible]	[illegible]	[illegible]	[illegible]
[illegible]	[illegible]	[illegible]			[illegible]	[illegible]	[illegible]	[illegible]
[illegible]	[illegible]	[illegible]	[illegible]		[illegible]	[illegible]	[illegible]	[illegible]
[illegible]	[illegible]	[illegible]	[illegible]	[illegible]	[illegible]	[illegible]	[illegible]	[illegible]
[illegible]	[illegible]	[illegible]	[illegible]	[illegible]	[illegible]	[illegible]	[illegible]	[illegible]
[illegible]	[illegible]	[illegible]	[illegible]	[illegible]	[illegible]	[illegible]	[illegible]	[illegible]
[illegible]	[illegible]	[illegible]	[illegible]	[illegible]	[illegible]	[illegible]	[illegible]	[illegible]
[illegible]	[illegible]	[illegible]	[illegible]	[illegible]	[illegible]	[illegible]	[illegible]	[illegible]
[illegible]	[illegible]	[illegible]	[illegible]	[illegible]	[illegible]	[illegible]	[illegible]	[illegible]
[illegible]	[illegible]	[illegible]	[illegible]	[illegible]	[illegible]	[illegible]	[illegible]	[illegible]
[illegible]	[illegible]	[illegible]	[illegible]	[illegible]	[illegible]	[illegible]	[illegible]	[illegible]
[illegible]	[illegible]	[illegible]	[illegible]	[illegible]	[illegible]	[illegible]	[illegible]	[illegible]
[illegible]	[illegible]	[illegible]	[illegible]	[illegible]	[illegible]	[illegible]	[illegible]	[illegible]
[illegible]	[illegible]	[illegible]	[illegible]	[illegible]	[illegible]	[illegible]	[illegible]	[illegible]
[illegible]	[illegible]	[illegible]	[illegible]	[illegible]	[illegible]	[illegible]	[illegible]	[illegible]
[illegible]	[illegible]	[illegible]	[illegible]	[illegible]	[illegible]	[illegible]	[illegible]	[illegible]
[illegible]	[illegible]				[illegible]	[illegible]	[illegible]	[illegible]
[illegible]	[illegible]	[illegible]	[illegible]	[illegible]	[illegible]	[illegible]	[illegible]	[illegible]
[illegible]	[illegible]	[illegible]	[illegible]	[illegible]	[illegible]	[illegible]	[illegible]	[illegible]
[illegible]	[illegible]	[illegible]			[illegible]	[illegible]	[illegible]	[illegible]
[illegible]	[illegible]	[illegible]	[illegible]	[illegible]	[illegible]	[illegible]	[illegible]	[illegible]
[illegible]	[illegible]	[illegible]	[illegible]	[illegible]	[illegible]	[illegible]	[illegible]	[illegible]
[illegible]	[illegible]	[illegible]			[illegible]	[illegible]	[illegible]	[illegible]
[illegible]	[illegible]	[illegible]	[illegible]	[illegible]	[illegible]	[illegible]	[illegible]	[illegible]
[illegible]	[illegible]	[illegible]	[illegible]	[illegible]	[illegible]	[illegible]	[illegible]	[illegible]
[illegible]	[illegible]	[illegible]	[illegible]	[illegible]	[illegible]	[illegible]	[illegible]	[illegible]
[illegible]	[illegible]	[illegible]	[illegible]	[illegible]	[illegible]	[illegible]	[illegible]	[illegible]
[illegible]	[illegible]	[illegible]			[illegible]	[illegible]	[illegible]	[illegible]
[illegible]	[illegible]	[illegible]	[illegible]	[illegible]	[illegible]	[illegible]	[illegible]	[illegible]
[illegible]	[illegible]	[illegible]	[illegible]	[illegible]	[illegible]	[illegible]	[illegible]	[illegible]
[illegible]	[illegible]	[illegible]	[illegible]	[illegible]	[illegible]	[illegible]	[illegible]	[illegible]
[illegible]	[illegible]	[illegible]	[illegible]	[illegible]	[illegible]	[illegible]	[illegible]	[illegible]
[illegible]	[illegible]	[illegible]	[illegible]	[illegible]	[illegible]	[illegible]	[illegible]	[illegible]

[illegible]	[illegible]	[illegible]		[illegible]	[illegible]	[illegible]	[illegible]	Mayo
[illegible]	[illegible]	[illegible]		[illegible]	[illegible]	[illegible]	[illegible]	Queen's County
[illegible]	[illegible]	[illegible]		[illegible]	[illegible]	[illegible]	[illegible]	Westmeath
[illegible]	[illegible]	[illegible]		[illegible]	[illegible]	[illegible]		Wexford
[illegible]	[illegible]	[illegible]		[illegible]	[illegible]	[illegible]		Wicklow
[illegible]	[illegible]	[illegible]	[illegible]	[illegible]	[illegible]	[illegible]	[illegible]	Total
								MUNSTER.
[illegible]	[illegible]	[illegible]		[illegible]	[illegible]	[illegible]		Clare
[illegible]	[illegible]	[illegible]	[illegible]	[illegible]	[illegible]	[illegible]	[illegible]	Cork
	[illegible]			[illegible]	[illegible]	[illegible]		Cork City
[illegible]	[illegible]	[illegible]	[illegible]	[illegible]	[illegible]	[illegible]		Kerry
[illegible]	[illegible]	[illegible]	[illegible]	[illegible]	[illegible]	[illegible]		Limerick
[illegible]	[illegible]	[illegible]		[illegible]	[illegible]	[illegible]		Limerick City
[illegible]	[illegible]	[illegible]		[illegible]	[illegible]	[illegible]		Tipperary
[illegible]	[illegible]	[illegible]		[illegible]	[illegible]	[illegible]		Waterford
				[illegible]	[illegible]	[illegible]		Waterford City and Suburbs
[illegible]	[illegible]	[illegible]	[illegible]	[illegible]	[illegible]	[illegible]	[illegible]	Total
								ULSTER.
[illegible]	[illegible]	[illegible]	[illegible]	[illegible]	[illegible]	[illegible]	[illegible]	Antrim
[illegible]	[illegible]	[illegible]		[illegible]	[illegible]	[illegible]		Armagh
				[illegible]	[illegible]	[illegible]		Carrickfergus [illegible]
[illegible]	[illegible]	[illegible]	[illegible]	[illegible]	[illegible]	[illegible]		Cavan
[illegible]	[illegible]	[illegible]	[illegible]	[illegible]	[illegible]	[illegible]	[illegible]	Donegal
[illegible]	[illegible]	[illegible]	[illegible]	[illegible]	[illegible]	[illegible]	[illegible]	Down
[illegible]	[illegible]	[illegible]	[illegible]	[illegible]	[illegible]	[illegible]		Fermanagh
[illegible]	[illegible]	[illegible]		[illegible]	[illegible]	[illegible]	[illegible]	Londonderry
				[illegible]	[illegible]	[illegible]		Londonderry City
[illegible]	[illegible]	[illegible]		[illegible]	[illegible]	[illegible]		Monaghan
[illegible]	[illegible]	[illegible]	[illegible]	[illegible]	[illegible]	[illegible]	[illegible]	Tyrone
[illegible]	[illegible]	[illegible]	[illegible]	[illegible]	[illegible]	[illegible]	[illegible]	Total

TABLE 64.—IRISH LAND COMMISSION.—Return of Sales to Tenants under the Purchase of Land (Ireland) Act, 1885, in which the Loans were issued during the year ending 31st August, 1888.

Provinces.	No. of Tenant Purchasers.	Purchase Money agreed upon.	Amount of Loans issued.	No. of Years' Purchase on Net Rental.
		£	£	
Ulster,	[illegible]	[illegible]	[illegible]	[illegible]
Munster,	[illegible]	[illegible]	[illegible]	[illegible]
Leinster,	[illegible]	[illegible]	[illegible]	[illegible]
Connaught,	[illegible]	[illegible]	[illegible]	[illegible]
Total,	[illegible]	[illegible]	[illegible]	[illegible]

RETURN of Sales to Tenants under the Purchase of Land (Ireland) Act, 1885, in which the Loans were issued during the period from 31st August, 1888, to 31st December, 1888.

Provinces.	No. of Tenant Purchasers.	Purchase Money agreed upon.	Amount of Loans issued.	No. of Years' Purchase on Net Rental.
		£	£	
Ulster,	[illegible]	[illegible]	[illegible]	[illegible]
Munster,	[illegible]	[illegible]	[illegible]	[illegible]
Leinster,	[illegible]	[illegible]	[illegible]	[illegible]
Connaught,	[illegible]	[illegible]	[illegible]	[illegible]
Total,	[illegible]	[illegible]	[illegible]	[illegible]

RETURN of Sales to Tenants under the Purchase of Land (Ireland) Act, 1885, in which the Loans were issued during the year ended 31st December, 1889.

Provinces.	No. of Tenant Purchasers.	Purchase Money agreed upon.	Amount of Loans issued.	No. of Years' Purchase on Net Rental.
		£	£	
Ulster,	[illegible]	[illegible]	[illegible]	[illegible]
Munster,	[illegible]	[illegible]	[illegible]	[illegible]
Leinster,	[illegible]	[illegible]	[illegible]	[illegible]
Connaught,	[illegible]	[illegible]	[illegible]	[illegible]
Total,	[illegible]	[illegible]	[illegible]	[illegible]

TABLE [illegible].—IRISH LAND COMMISSION.—Return of Sales to Tenants under the Purchase of Land (Ireland) Act, [illegible], in which Loans were issued during the Year ending the 31st December, [illegible]

Province.	No. of Tenant Purchasers	Purchase Money agreed upon	Amount of Loans sanctioned	No. of Years' Purchase on Net Rental
		£	£	
Ulster,	[illegible]	[illegible]	[illegible]	[illegible]
Munster,	[illegible]	[illegible]	[illegible]	[illegible]
Leinster,	[illegible]	[illegible]	[illegible]	[illegible]
Connaught,	[illegible]	[illegible]	[illegible]	[illegible]
Total	[illegible]	[illegible]	[illegible]	[illegible]

TABLE [illegible].—TABLE showing the NUMBER of EVICTION NOTICES FILED in the HIGH COURT of JUSTICE and COUNTY COURTS in IRELAND, under SECTION [illegible] of the LAND LAW (IRELAND) ACT, [illegible], during the year [illegible]

—	Notices Filed
Queen's Bench Division,	[illegible]
Exchequer Division,	[illegible]
County Courts,	[illegible]
Total,	[illegible]

DUBLIN CASTLE,

6th September, 1895.

SIR,

I have to acknowledge the receipt of your letter of the 2nd instant, forwarding, for submission to His Excellency the Lord Lieutenant, your Report on the Criminal and Judicial Statistics of Ireland for the year 1894.

I am, Sir,

Your obedient Servant,

D. HARREL.

The Registrar General,

Charlemont House,

Rutland Square.

www.ingramcontent.com/pod-product-compliance
Lightning Source LLC
Chambersburg PA
CBHW021810190326
41518CB00007B/537